GUY
TOWN
—— BY ——
GASLIGHT

GUY TOWN

BY

GASLIGHT

A HISTORY OF
VICE IN AUSTIN'S FIRST WARD

RICHARD ZELADE

Charleston · London

THE
History
PRESS

Published by The History Press
Charleston, SC 29403
www.historypress.net

Copyright © 2014 by Richard Zelade
All rights reserved

Cover images: Pressler's Garden ad from an Austin city directory, courtesy of Edwin O.
Wilson; back cover photo courtesy of Spoiled Doves of Texas, Art Nunes, photographer.

First published 2014

Manufactured in the United States

ISBN 978.1.62619.445.8

Library of Congress CIP data applied for.

CONTENTS

PREFACE

Guy Town by Gaslight *may never grace the title page of a modern romance, but the scene there last night would be a fine ground work for a novel by Alexander Dumas.*
—Austin Daily Statesman, *November 6, 1881*

Parents, keep your boys off of the streets at night. A city under the gaslight is quite a different thing from a city under the sunlight.
—Austin Daily Statesman, *November 8, 1881*

Guy Town was Austin's red-light district, located in old Austin's First Ward, which is now the uber-trendy Warehouse District. The First Ward was bounded by Congress Avenue on the east, West Avenue on the west, Pecan Street on the north and the Colorado River on the south. Guy Town's heyday lasted about fifteen years, from 1881 to 1895.

I've known about Guy Town for than half of my life, and having visited several "Boys' Towns" along the Texas/Mexico border, I knew what transpired there, but my interest was not aroused until I began researching the history of early railroading in Austin. As I read old Austin newspapers on microfilm, hour after hour, day after day, year after year, I couldn't help but notice the chronicle of life in Guy Town and its relation to the railroads. I learned intimate life details of dozens of outrageous characters. Reporting was different back then. Reporters were more like storytellers, and the goings-on in Guy Town were their creative inkwell. If John Steinbeck had lived in Austin, he would have

written *Guy Town by Gaslight,* and it would be treasured like *Cannery Row* and *Tortilla Flats* are today. I'm no John Steinbeck, but I'm going to try to do a pretty fair job of entertaining you with the stories of Guy Town as they really happened.

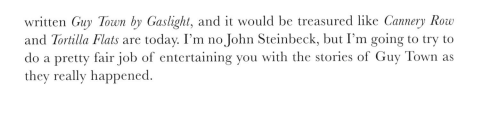

Opposite, top: Aerial view of Guy Town, 1887. *From* Austin, State Capital of Texas, *drawn by August Koch, 1887. Author's collection.*

Opposite, bottom: Looking down on Guy Town. *Courtesy of the Austin History Center.*

CHAPTER 1

IN THE BEGINNING

"Texas is a heaven for men and dogs but hell for women and oxen," goes the old saying. Texas was hell for prostitutes as well, until after the Civil War. Prior to war's end, references to prostitutes in Texas were as scarce as hen's teeth; in 1862, a man filed for divorce because his wife had left his bed and board and become a prostitute.

The Union army was prostitution's best friend; wherever Yankee soldiers went, hookers followed. When Union soldiers entered Texas at war's end, so did the rent girls. Galveston, the port of entry for the army of occupation, was ground zero. By the fall of 1865, Galveston's city council had passed ordinances aimed at controlling prostitution and other forms of vice.

Austin, born in 1839, had gamblers and drunkards from day one, but we didn't have a proper whore, soiled dove, cyprian, *fille de joie*, frail one, *nymph du pave*, cull on the hoof, *demimonde*, rent girl, local, *chere ami*, courtesan, virago—call her what you will—until after the Civil War.

Union troops raised the Stars and Stripes over Austin on June 16, 1865. And thus, the seeds for what would eventually become Guy Town were sown.

We do not know when the first whore came to Austin, when the first whorehouse opened or when Austin's First Ward began to coalesce as the sin district that came to be called Guy Town, except that nothing seemed out of the ordinary on October 30, 1867, when a newspaper reporter took a ride through west Austin, including the First Ward, and noted that freedmen who had come to Austin to seek their happiness as well as their bread "amid the pleasures" of city life were building quite a number of shacks.

"Taking a Break." *Author's collection.*

"Seeking Their Happiness." *Author's collection.*

Thus began the life of a low-rent district. Low-rent neighborhoods naturally attracted poor people: immigrants, laborers, widows, musicians, actors, gamblers, thieves, con artists and other assorted ne'er-do-wells. Drunkenness was common; men and women drank themselves into unconsciousness to escape their misery for a few hours. Yes, women. Some gals could drink almost any man under the table. But if you passed out for the night on the sidewalk or in other public place, the police would scoop you in and charge you five dollars and costs, which was almost a week's wages.

The saloons served cheap drinks, and the hundreds of occupying Union soldiers didn't earn much, so when they got their monthly pay, they headed for the First Ward, where they quite enjoyed themselves. The police made periodic sweeps of the gambling rooms and saloons, but whorehouses were never mentioned.

The First Ward became Austin's most racially and ethnically diverse neighborhood. An 1875 city census lists nearly 200 Mexicans. "Coloreds" numbered about 250. "Americans" hovered around 150, while there were several dozens each of Germans and Italians and lesser numbers of Irish, English, Poles, French, Scots, Swedes and "Israelites"; there were even 16 Chinese, who, according to the stereotype of the time, were launderers.

At about eleven o'clock on the morning of June 30, 1869, the sound of a pistol shot from a small house located behind a large stone shop on Colorado Street startled the denizens of the neighborhood that would become known as Guy Town, which already had two or three houses occupied by white women of the *demimonde* persuasion, gamblers and idle persons generally. The houses were usually quiet, yet their neighbors considered the houses a nuisance and would have been glad to get rid of them.

A company of all colors, sexes and ages at once assembled outside the house. In a small room immediately on the alley, a policeman guarded the door, and inside were Justice Scott, six jury men of the inquest, a lawyer, a physician and two or three white and black women of the place. On a small bed in the corner, lying on her back, her body covered with a sheet and her face exposed, was the lifeless form of Laura Lensing, seemingly asleep. Meanwhile, Jack Connor, the accused, was walking the yard, proclaiming that it had been an accident. A pistol shot had entered Laura's right side and penetrated her body. She was just twenty-three years old. Connor was convicted in November for killing her and sentenced to five years in the state pen.

By the summer of 1870, Austin (population: 4,400) was inching its way into the ranks of a proper city, but it was still a frontier town in many ways,

"Gunfighters." *From Sketches from* Texas Siftings, *Sweet and Knox, S.W. Green's Son, 1882.*

lacking a railroad or river transport, paved streets, streetcars, a water system, streetlamps, sewers or garbage collection. Men shot up one another all over town. Cattle drives passed up Congress Avenue.

Austin's budding vice district now had a name, or rather, several variations: Ebron, Ebron yard and Ebronville. In the King James Bible, Ebron was a misspelling of Hebron, the second-most sacred city of Israel, believed to have been home to Adam and Eve after their expulsion from Eden; the city where Cain killed Abel; home to Abraham and David; the city where Abraham's wife, Sarah, died; and possibly the birthplace of John the Baptist. However, in fact, Ebronville was the namesake of Thomas Ebron, who died on January 5, 1871, at the age of forty-five. He had accumulated quite a handsome estate, including the plot that bore his name.

After the Lensing tragedy, times in "Ebron" got wilder. On the evening of July 29, 1870, a state policeman went to a "favorite resort of the colored population for gambling purposes," where he arrested a wanted man. But his prisoner broke and ran, the policeman in pursuit. Friends of the escapee fired two shots, one grazing the side of the officer's head, and this so stunned him that the prisoner escaped.

One week later, another unnamed man was fined for bandying epithets with one of the "frail creatures." Later that night, a "couple of families of the colored persuasion" got into a row and "made the wool and clothes fly." The police arrested the whole party—big, little, old, young—and placed them in the calaboose, all in a lump. They were convicted and fined according to the degree of their offences.

On August 8, two soldiers and a citizen were arrested and convicted for disorderly conduct; two black men for raising a row at a ball; and two black women for pulling each other's hair. All of this caused the *Tri-Weekly State Gazette* to despair on August 12, 1870:

> *Ebronville must be the five points of Austin if we may judge from reports and the number of arrests made there. Nearly every case tried has been from that quarter. Westley Stewart and John Williams were engaged in a row at Ebronville and assessed five dollars and costs for their amusement. Stewart paid and was released, but Williams not having the herewith, was taken in by the police. The repose of Wednesday night was broken by a hideous row in a negro bagnio, between all sorts of colors. Shots were exchanged, but no one was hurt. The police entered the place, and arrested nearly a score of noisy offenders. We need a workhouse for such gentry.*

Seven soldiers were also brought before the Mayor's Court for disturbing the peace by raising a muss. They all paid the mandated price for their fun, but their commanding officer told city officials that it was okay to put them to work on the street instead.

Harry Williams, a soldier, stabbed Isaac Wheat, a black man, at Ebron yard on Friday, September 2, 1870, about dark. Wheat's bowels protruded some distance and presented a sickening sight. Williams attempted to escape but was arrested and was lodged in jail after considerable resistance.

Then, for unknown reasons, everything quieted down for a few days. "What is the matter?" the *Gazette* marveled on September 7. "Only one poor dilapidated individual, since last Saturday, has offered himself as a sacrifice to sustain the dignity of the city. Verily, we are becoming a pious people. Our police can now lazily doze and dream of days gone by, when Ebronville was in all its glory, and a drunk or row peeped out at every corner. But ah! The halcyon days are

"Pulling the Wool." *From* On a Mexican Mustang through Texas: From the Gulf to the Rio Grande, *Sweet and Knox, Chatto and Windus, Piccadilly, 1884.*

over for a time. It was no more trouble to obtain a first class local then than it is now to loan a friend a quarter. We can only live now in the hope of a glorious future. The Solons [legislators] will soon return, and with their advent, locals will abound, and Mayor and police resume their usual smiles."

That "poor dilapidated individual" was a burglar who entered the home of James M. Simms, at the corner of Cypress and Guadalupe. Simms's daughter, awakening in the night, discovered a man sitting by her bedside. She immediately screamed, whereupon he attempted to choke her, but her father rushed in and the villain sprang to the window, leaped out and made his escape, leaving his hat by the window, his belt on the bed and his shoes on the outside. Owing to the bright moonlight, Simms and his daughter easily recognized the scoundrel. He was soon captured and in jail. And thus began James Simms's campaign to clean up the First Ward, which would finally end in tragedy ten years later.

The 1870 census offered no clues as to which enumerated women were prostitutes, so we can only guess at the number by looking at arrest reports in the newspapers of the day. Only a handful of women, like repeat offender Cerilda Miller, were outright identified as *demimondes*, but considering the charges leveled against certain women—such as fighting, offensive language and drunkenness—and nicknames like "Bow-legged Liz," a guess of twelve to fifteen during the early 1870s is not too bad. In 1875, the Chinese may very well have outnumbered the madams and prostitutes. Good cases can be made against about fifteen women as being professional "ceiling starers," based on arrest records, where they lived and if they were living in the same house together with young ladies of approximately the same age with no means of support listed except perhaps that of seamstress. Ida Lake, whose notoriety would last late into the 1880s, was listed as a seamstress in 1875, as were some of the girls who were living with Sallie Daggett.

Despite the attempts of Simms and the "decent" folk to clean up the First Ward, the neighborhood continued its dive into depravity, thanks in no small part to "Mexican Charley" Cunio (or Cuneo or Cooney or Cuny or Cuney).

Marshal M.M. Long received information that a murder had been committed in a house near Charley's store early one evening in May 1874. He broke down the door and found John Raphael withering in his gore, his front teeth knocked in and his skull broken by an axe or other heavy weapon. Those around indicated that an Italian living close by was responsible. He was immediately arrested and jailed.

By January 31, 1875, the *Statesman* had declared that "Five Points," sometimes called "Mexico," was about the dirtiest, roughest corner of creation laid down on the city map, and Marshal Ed Creary had his eye on that portion of Austin.

Things were lively down in "Cooneyville," on Sunday, July 27, 1875. A black man, "Wild Bill," got into a fracas with Giuseppi Morizzio, an Italian saloonkeeper. Morizzio got a dangerous knife wound under the ear, and a lively race ensued to catch Wild Bill, who was caught while climbing a fence and was soon after lodged in jail.

Another row occurred between Mack Horst, a prominent black "sporting man," and a Mexican. They exchanged several pistol shots, without effect. The Mexicans gathered in force, and Horst ran like a horse to escape their vengeance. This race was about as exciting as the other. "Cooneyville" (or "Five Points" or "Mexico" or whatever name the place was known by) had gained a reputation as a hard corner, and bad whiskey was said to be remarkably plentiful thereabouts.

All of this was enough for James Simms, who moved out of the First Ward around September 1, 1875, into the more respectable seventh ward. Judge Sneed and other "respectable" folk were also compelled to vacate the first, at heavy sacrifice.

Charley's unpopularity was such that when, later that month, he filed assault and battery charges against John Roggio, a Pecan Street merchant, the following extraordinary verdict was rendered: "We, the jury, find the plaintiff [Cunio] a nuisance to the city corporation, and subject to all the costs in this suit. The defendant is honorably acquitted."

The city council passed an ordinance in November 1875 that dancing should not be allowed at houses of prostitution, where prostitutes congregate or where such house or place is attached or belongs to any drinking saloon, as well as that any party violating the ordinance shall be fined not less than $5 nor more than $100. The ordinance was aimed in large part at Charley. In February 1876, some unknown parties started firing shots into the doors and windows of a respectable First Ward residence. No officers were within hearing to arrest them, and they kept shooting until their pistols were emptied. Only one officer was detailed for that part of the city, and all his energies were required to keep the peace at Charley's store.

In another attempt to control the First Ward, the city council passed an ordinance in March 1876 defining and providing the punishment for vagrants:

A vagrant is hereby declared to be an idle person, living without any means of support, and making no exertions to obtain a livelihood by honest employment. All persons who stroll about to tell fortunes or to exhibit tricks or cheats in public, not licensed by law, common prostitutes and professional gamblers, or persons who keep houses for prostitutes or for gamblers; persons who go about begging for alms (and who are not afflicted or disabled by physical malady or misfortune); and habitual drunkards, who abandon, neglect or refuse to aid in the support of their families, and who may be complained of by their families; or persons who stroll idly about the streets of this city, having no local habitation, and no honest business or employment, each and all of the above and aforesaid classes be and are hereby declared vagrants, coming within the meaning of this ordinance.

Any person guilty of being a vagrant in this city shall be guilty of a misdemeanor, and shall be fined, not to exceed ten dollars.

Despite its notoriety, the First Ward played a deciding role in local elections. On October 28, 1875, the *Statesman* fumed:

Mayor Wheeler's friends are busy naturalizing and registering voters, and of the 18 or 20 police, detectives, or what not, under the pay of the city, a large number seem to be on the general staff, that is, are working where they can do the most good—politically. This is only one of the many expedients used by a desperate political trickster to defeat the will of the people at the ballot box. The Mayor's speech at "Mexico" on Tuesday night was full of the lowest appeals to the passions of the rabble. And all this from a young man who was elected to the high position he holds, but does not fill, by the vote of the Democracy two short years ago.

All the arts of the great cities and corrupt practices of debased Tammanies are practiced here in Austin. All sorts of roughs are being imported, and strangers are rapidly naturalized and furnished with registrars' certificates, and 500 plug uglies may be boarded at the public expense from this time till Monday next. Therefore the knaves of all Texas gather in each town about election times. The candidates feed and whisky them, and thus taxpayers are robbed by roughs, and therefore the people should see to it that vicious-looking strangers, on election day, are kept away from voting places.

Make your own guess as to which part of town hosted those "plug uglies."

Election shenanigans in Guy Town merited a "joke" in an 1884 issue of *Texas Siftings*, the country's leading weekly humor publication (for anyone offended by the "n" word, please skip over this passage):

It was late in the afternoon of a local election day in Austin. A prominent candidate asked one of his strikers [an election blackmailer] *if he had voted an insane old negro who lived in Guyton* [Guy Town], *a suburb of Austin.*

"Yes I voted him once but the opposition got him away from me and they have been voting him ever since."

"Why that's an outrage," shrieked the candidate. "It's against the law for them to vote a crazy nigger."

"I know it," replied the striker, "but I can't get him away from them now. Anyhow, we will make a big fuss about it, if we are beaten."

In 1902, the poll tax became a requirement for voting, effectively disenfranchising blacks, Mexican Americans and poor whites, the culmination of a decades-long campaign by "respectable" Texans to keep the "knaves, roughs, and rabble" from defeating "the will of the people" at the ballot box.

On May 11, 1876, the *Statesman* railed:

Before members of the Legislature vote upon an amendment to the Constitution regarding local suffrage in towns and cities, they should get a guide and "go through" that part of Austin known as "Mexico" or "Five Points," but we would advise them to take a body guard along and to leave all their valuables and important bills and State papers at their respective hasheries. They should visit all of Tom Hill's domiciles—a host of shanties rented to all sorts and complexions of people who live like prairie dogs, owls and snakes in the Pan Handle lands of Texas. Tom is a negro capitalist who rents houses for a living, and, like many of his race, and whites as well, he don't care how much he injures other people so long as he gets his rents at the end of the month. Tom and his tenants come in heavy about election time, and will support anyone that will wink at "ways that are dark and tricks that are in vain" down in "Mexico." By all means let the Legislature go through the first ward of the State capital and then take home to themselves the question, "Have taxpayers and respectable, law-abiding people any rights that legislators are under obligation to respect." It is all wrong that towns and cities should be turned over to the rabble by universal as well as fraudulent voting, and we mildly suggest that some legislator can immortalize himself by securing the passage of a bill which will bring a stop to this state of things in Texas.

"The Texas Legislature." *From* On a Mexican Mustang through Texas: From the Gulf to the Rio Grande, *Sweet and Knox, Chatto and Windus, Piccadilly, 1884.*

Members of the legislature were already regular visitors to "Mexico." On May 21, 1876, the *Statesman* reported that "[t]wo women, charged by the city with keeping a disreputable house, threaten to tell who are their most frequent visitors, and several high-toned gentlemen are trembling in their boots." At the same time, the *Statesman* complained that more policemen were needed and that the council should get the city's finances in such a shape as to justify the multiplication of the force.

Many of the officers proved to be no better than those they policed. One night in July 1876, a few officers indulged in a little "set-to." "That was bad example," the *Statesman* scolded, "and when they may arrest someone for fighting hereafter, no doubt their minds will be refreshed about their own reprehensible conduct."

Many of the officers showed extreme discretion in their arrests. On November 11, 1877, the *Statesman* complained, "Some of the gay and festive made the First Ward roar last Monday night by the keen crack of their six shooters. If it were not for these fellows who loaf around the street wearing blue clothes, with whistle and club, the city would be in a bad fix; yet they are not very ready in tackling street rowdies, but if they catch an unfortunate country fellow they waltz him off at a rate that is refreshing to behold."

They gave especially wide berth to Ben Thompson, the "Colossus of Austin," who often took target practice down in "Mexico" before he was elected city marshal of Austin in 1880, to the extent that the *Statesman* reported in September 1878:

> *Ben Thompson says that since the city authorities have decided that they have no penalty in their book of ordinances against fire-arms, and discharging the same in the streets, he will quit turning the blessed retreat called "Mexico" into a nocturnal shooting gallery. The sport lost zest with Ben when it became a matter that no longer concerned the police. Ben agrees with most men that "forbidden fruit is the sweetest."*

And again on November 9, 1878:

> *If it takes a dozen policemen and three or four deputy sheriffs to arrest a 14 year old boy charged with stealing $7, how many thousand officers of the same sort would it take to arrest Ben Thompson for firing off his pistol in a public place?*

When Deputy Sheriff Rudolph Krause refused to arrest Ben Thompson for one of his escapades, deeming it prudent to let Ben surrender on his own terms (as he always did, for Ben was an honorable man), Krause was fired on the spot.

The "countrymen" who visited "Mexico" included sheriffs from distant and not-so-distant parts of the state, who likewise deemed it prudent to go heavily armed at all times and places.

"We assure them that our citizens, as a class, are eminently peaceable, and if they shun evil company and steer clear of the places that are dark, they are as safe as if under their own vine and fig tree," the *Statesman* counseled.

> *But, alas, there's the rub. Nearly all of them seem to consider it absolutely necessary to their very existence to arm themselves to the teeth and visit*

places of dangerous and unenvied repute [where] *they nearly always drink to excess and are ready to go off like a shot at any real or imaginary insult, and quicker than nine shakes of a sheep's tail they draw their arms and bloodshed follows. The other night an officer visiting the city went down into the first ward, and as a matter of course, drinking to excess, waxed pot-valiant and drew his six-shooter, and had not a policeman promptly reached the spot and disarmed him, it is more than probable the city would have been shocked the next morning with the startling news that another murder had been committed, and per chance an innocent person hurried into eternity. For the sake of society, if not for their own welfare and reputations, we respectfully advise officers of the law, when visiting the city on peaceable errands, to lay aside their arms.*

It was advice that Palo Pinto County sheriff Wilson and Marshal Ball of Sherman should have heeded on the evening of January 23, 1879. Ball made a remark that offended Wilson, pistols were drawn, shots were exchanged and Wilson fell dead in the street.

And the low life went on as usual in the "fighting first." Officer John Chenneville arrested Daisy Compton and Nettie Hoffmann on September 16, 1879, for stealing $190 from John Dixon, a Kansas cattleman. He had stepped off the train and into "Mexico." With $190 in his pocket, and under the influence of mean whiskey, he felt immensely wealthy and was having a high old time with Daisy and Nettie until he fell into a deep sleep. While in this condition, he was relieved of all his money. When he recovered his senses and found his money gone, he made a complaint against the two delectable females, resulting in their arrest.

Then, on March 11, 1880, a sort of watershed event occurred in one of "Mexico's" lowliest watering holes, the Gem Saloon. James Simms Jr., son of the man who had led the unsuccessful fight to halt the First Ward's descent into sin, was shot to death in a gambling row. (His death is detailed in "Fakir, Taker," a later chapter.)

On March 13, the name "Guy Town" first appeared in print, and although folks would continue to refer to the area as "Mexico," "Cooneyville" and the First Ward, the mantle had been passed.

CHAPTER 2
WHAT'S IN A NAME?

That's when I want
Some weird sin
Just to relax with,
For awhile, anyway
—"Some Weird Sin," Iggy Pop

Guy Town" was where Victorian-era Austinites relaxed with their dumb, weird sins. Victorian-age Americans indulged in pretty much any sexual practice you can think of nowadays. Just Google something like "Victorian prostitute images," and you'll eyeball the same wide variety of pleasuring positions, innovative use of furniture, fellatio, threesomes, gangbangs, lesbian and gay recontres, vibrators and rubber devices suitable for vaginal or anal insertion. The chief differences are that the women tended to be a bit chunkier than they are now (like Frank Zappa once said, "The bigger the cushion, the better the pushin'"), and both men and women sported more body hair in the appropriate places than today.

A handful of Guy Town's spoiled doves might be considered beauties by today's standards, but most of today's prized lovelies would have been scorned back in Guy Town's heyday as scrawny and probably fatally ill with the consumption. "Grade A" gals commonly weighed 170, perhaps even 200 pounds. The chubby side of life was considered to be a mark of health in those days. Rotund men and plump women enjoyed great respect. It took money to eat enough to get fat, money that the average American lacked.

Cutting-edge sexual practices seem to have been largely absent from Guy Town bordellos. There is no evidence of cathouses offering gay or lesbian specialties. You went to Storyville in New Orleans for that sort of pleasuring. Not that sodomy and buggery didn't take place in Victorian Austin—one incidence of each was recorded in the *Statesman*.

Austin was the capital of Texas, but Guy Town was rather minor league when compared with the great red-light districts in New York City, Chicago and San Antonio, with their "gilded palaces of sin." San Antonio's ten-block "Sporting District" counted more than one hundred places where you could have a good time; Guy Town sported only a few dozen in a similarly sized area.

Guy Town's "gilded palaces of sin" consisted of a bare handful of fashionable gingerbread wood-frame mansions. As the *Statesman* stated on April 23, 1886:

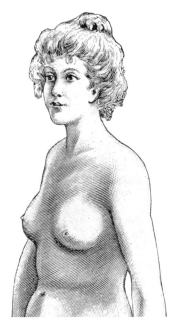

"Victorian Beauty." *From* Harter's Picture Archive for Collage Illustrations, *Jim Harter, Dover Publications.*

> *Between the depot and the railroad bridge on the west there are a number of miserable shanties to which the vilest characters of the city resort. They have been the hatching places of more than one deed of crime and blood. They are moral cancers on the body of the good city of Austin. They are within the legal definition of disorderly houses, because they are kept up for uses and purposes which the law condemns; they are nuisances, because of their being crammed to repletion with every conceivable sort of filth. Public decency, and public health, alike, demand their abatement. The city authorities are invited to go and see if the picture is overdrawn.*

The only reference to one of those "gilded palaces" here came on March 19, 1894, when the *Statesman* reported that a certain local gentleman had roamed up against the gilded palace of sin of Miss Georgia Fraser and, not exactly liking the way things were being run, attempted to rid the house of two of its inmates by sending them by the pistol bullet route to

Georgia Fraser's bagnio. *Courtesy of Austin History Center.*

the another world, but the girls being active and his aim being bad, they escaped without injury.

Unlike many other cities that had regulated vice districts, Guy Town had no official boundaries. Sporting houses and variety theaters of ill repute were also found east of Congress Avenue, as were "houses of assignation," where married women and their lovers could pay a dollar or two to tryst for an hour or the night.

We do not know the details about the nocturnal "scene" that inspired the quote that, in turn, inspired the name for this book, but chances are that it involved a whore and a john, given that Dumas' famous novel and play, *Camille*, vividly described an ill-fated love affair between a beautiful and brazen young courtesan suffering from tuberculosis and a young, provincial bourgeois man. Sexually charged women were thought especially susceptible to "consumption," as TB was then called. Camille died alone and in agony, as did many of Austin's soiled doves during Guy Town's heyday.

The only ruckus we know of occurred about midnight, at the corner of Congress Avenue and Pecan Street. A black man was at a late-night stand partaking of chili con carne y tamales when another black man pushed him into the mud. The soiled party arose and went for the other fellow. A mêlée ensued, and Officer Holland interfered to restore peace. He was knocked down by the man who caused the original disturbance. Holland recovered and whopped the man several times with his "billy," but the surrounding crowd was too much for him. Holland was struck several times and left quite bloody.

City elections were then coming up in a little more than twenty-four hours. Bribing prospective voters of all races and ethnicities with liberal doses of liquor was a common election tactic, and the black vote was ardently courted by many white candidates. A number of "boisterous darkies" threatened to "fix that officer" before daylight, the *Statesman* reported, "but it was election whiskey that was talking, and they did nothing."

Guy Town by Gaslight is a riff on the title of George G. Foster's *New York by Gas-Light* (1850), which explored "the festivities of prostitution, the orgies of pauperism, the haunts of theft and murder, the scenes of drunkenness and beastly debauch, and all the sad realities that go to make up the lower stratum—the underground story—of life in New York!" Foster, a *New York Tribune* reporter, drew on his rambles through the city's streets and among the *demimondes* to produce an extraordinarily revealing portrait of contemporary New York:

> *"Five Points"…is, indeed, a sad, an awful sight. Here, whence these streets diverge in dark and endless paths, whose steps take hold on hell—here is the very type and physical semblance, in fact, of hell itself.*
>
> *It is no unusual thing for a mother and her two or three daughters—all of course prostitutes—to receive their "men" at the same time and in the same room—passing in and out and going through all the transaction of their hellish intercourse, with a sang froid at which devils would stand aghast and struck with horror.*

Guy Town was full of such dark and endless paths whose steps took hold on hell.

Austinites had a healthy fear of the dark. From 1839 until 1872, Austin had relied on moonlight, candles and torches to light the night. The night darkness was fraught with danger, from early-day Indian ambushes to falls, assaults, robberies and murder. Nowhere was safe.

AUSTIN GAS LIGHT

and

COAL CO.,

ALL ORDERS FOR

GAS, COAL, COKE and COAL TAR,

Should be addressed to

A. E. JUDGE, *Superintendent,*

Or left at the Works, south east corner Live Oak
and Colorado Streets.

Complaints should be made directly to the Superintendent or sent through the Mail.

From Mooney & Morrison's General Directory of the City of Austin, Texas, for 1877–78,
Houston. *Courtesy E.O. Wilson.*

On the evening of February 19, 1873, someone robbed and fatally stabbed
state representative Louis Franke on the steps of the state capitol. The perp had
probably intended to kill and rob Mr. Rhodes, sergeant at arms of the House.
Rhodes had drawn the per diem money of a large number of House members
that day and even after dark was carrying several thousand dollars, not yet
delivered. Franke was of the same frame and height as Rhodes, wore his beard
somewhat similarly and may have been mistaken in the dark for Rhodes.

It is little wonder that Austinites were so adamant about getting street
lamps. "What has become of the proposition to light Austin with gas?" the
Austin Statesman pleaded after the Franke killing. "If the city was lighted as
it should be, assassinations could not be made in the most public places."
Three years earlier, the *Tri-Weekly State Gazette* had begged the question, "It
is reported there are burglars and pickpockets in our city. Will not our city
fathers have lamps put upon the Avenue and principal streets?"

The Austin Gas Company was organized in July 1871, and one year later, the major streets sported lights. But after just two months in operation, the company cut off the gas because the city failed to pay its bill. Austin's gas streetlights were shining again by the summer of 1874—on Congress Avenue at least. Much of the city, including Guy Town, was still in the dark.

Austin was on a boom then; its population more than doubled between 1870 and 1880. Yet in February 1878, the city council reduced the city's oil street lamps from sixty-nine to twenty-five, leaving the outer wards in utter darkness. Oil lamps were necessary because the gas mains did not extend beyond downtown. Citizens living in the First Ward and elsewhere experienced much difficulty in reaching their homes after dark. "There would be less burglary, horse stealing and other crime in these localities if there were more lamps," the *Statesman* editorialized on May 5, 1878. The streetlights went unlit during the full moon as long as the nights were not cloudy.

Guy Town was the last in a series of names given to Austin's sin-tertainment district, beginning with Ebron, Ebron yard or Ebronville (circa 1870), Five Points (circa 1870), Mexico (circa 1873), Cooneyville (circa 1875) and the First Ward.

Guy Town was home to elegant mansions, miserable shacks and hovels, whorehouses, saloons, gambling joints, lunch stands, boardinghouses, stores,

The old one-room schoolhouse. *Author's collection.*

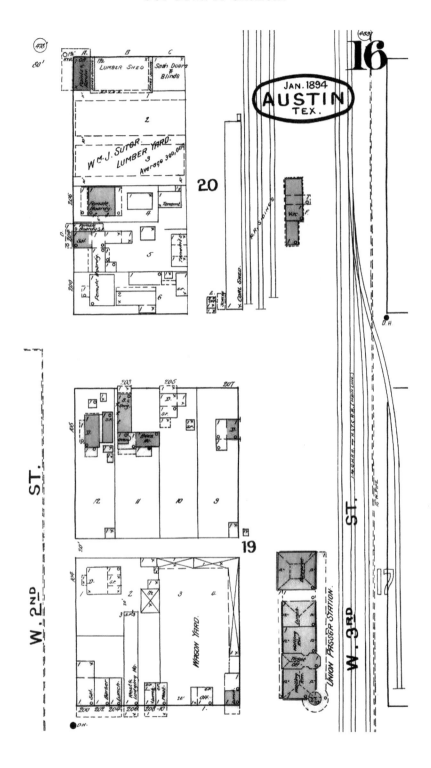

Opposite: An 1894 Sanborn fire insurance map of the train station neighborhood. "Female boardinghouses" were only a kiss away.

Left: "The Drummer, Just in from St. Louis and Looking for a Good Time." *From Sketches from* Texas Siftings, *Sweet and Knox, S.W. Green's Son, 1882.*

restaurants, factories, a garbage dump and the train station. Horny after that two-day trip from St. Louis? A short walk rewarded you with a choice of three "female boardinghouses" and a saloon if you wanted to take the plunge with a full tank. The ubiquitous one-room city schoolhouse four blocks away was surrounded by tenements.

Rich families lived around the corner from vagrants. Two mayors came from the First Ward: Thomas B. Wheeler (1872–77) and William Saylor (1881–84). Wheeler owned quite a bit of the ward's slum property, and his tenants included a number of prostitutes. Wheeler would go on to serve as lieutenant governor of Texas (1887–91). The ward's major industries included two wood-planing mills (Cedar at San Antonio); the Austin Gas Light and Coal Company plant (Live Oak between Congress and Colorado), which kept the streetlights and home lamps lit; and two ice factories.

There were no churches in Guy Town, but tent and open-air meetings often attracted large congregations. Denizens from the notorious dives would sit outside the enclosure listening to the words of love and mercy as they fell from the lips of the earnest preacher.

Above: Easy pickings. *From the* Social Survey of Austin, *issue 15, of* Bulletin of the University of Texas, *issue 273, William Benjamin Hamilton, University of Texas, 1913. Courtesy E.O. Wilson.*

Opposite, top: From Mooney & Morrison's General Directory of the City of Austin, Texas, for 1877–78, Houston. *Courtesy E.O. Wilson.*

Opposite, bottom: J.P. Schneider Building. *Author's collection.*

Only one Guy Town–era building remains: the Schneider Building at Second and Guadalupe, once part of the Schneider wagon yard and store complex.

No one knows who coined the name "Guy Town." It first appeared in print on March 13, 1880. At about three o'clock the previous morning, pistol shots were heard in the vicinity of "Guy Town," the *Austin Statesman* reported. Officers Johnson, Chenneville and Watts arrived promptly on the spot but could not ascertain who did the shooting. They met, however, two young men—sons of prominent citizens, who moved in the best circles of society—one of whom had figured in the Mayor's Court some time earlier for firing off a pistol on Pine Street. The officers believed that these lamb-like gents had done the shooting.

Did the reporter repeat a name he had heard on the streets, or did he coin "Guy Town" himself? Within Guy Town were savory sub-localities like Tin

Cup Alley, Clabber Alley, Dirty Row and Greasy Row. But then, the rest of Austin was pretty filthy too. Grocers, restaurateurs and bartenders threw their trash into the gutters that lined both sides of Congress Avenue. During the summer of 1881, an old motherly-looking cow passed down Congress Avenue every morning picking up scraps of melons and bits of potato and hay. Folks often saw this cow staggering down the street, intoxicated from the effects of eating pieces of lemons thrown out of the saloons. Half-starved, ragged little children roamed the streets daily, picking up filthy watermelon rinds, rotten apples, potatoes and so on, all of which they ate "with all the relish a pig would display," according to one paper.

Then there were the dogs; on the morning of July 31, 1881, there was much complaint about the large number of dead dogs lying about the streets, filling the atmosphere with the most horrible odors. The dog killer had commenced his rampage in Guy Town a few days earlier, when eight dead dogs were hauled off.

The pelon, or "Mexican hairless dog," was the national dog of Guy Town. The average pelon was of a purple-blue color, with bandy legs, and was always fat, the result of an advantage he had over all other dogs: he was as bald as the inside of a goose, with the exception of two tufts of hair sprouting out between his ears. He was not troubled, as other curs were, by detachments of fleas scouting over him and therefore did not keep himself thin with the exercise of scratching his left ear with his right hind leg.

Pelon, the "Mexican hairless dog." *From* Sketches from Texas Siftings, *Sweet and Knox, S.W. Green's Son, 1882.*

Strangers from the East, who never saw a pelon until they came to Austin, were puzzled considerably when they saw the naked dog for the first time. A Chicago man, just arrived in Austin, asked the baggage man at the depot what "the matter [was] with that dog?" The baggage man was busy and replied, in the pleasant, laconic manner of baggage men when they are busy, "Coal-oil lamp explosion." The Chicago man was surprised as he walked up town to see two or three dogs on every block with their hair apparently singed entirely off them.

Meeting the baggage man at the hotel door, he remarked, "Say, mister, didn't…didn't the coal-oil lamp explode in a dog factory?"

But back to the origins of the name. The "Guy" part had come over from England a few years earlier, deriving from Guy Fawkes, leader of a failed Catholic revolt against King James I in 1605. Some have said that "guy" was a contemporary slang word for a prostitute, but there is no surviving newspaper or other written account to support the claim.

The most likely explanation has to do with the Victorian-era meaning of "guy." A guy was an object of ridicule—a man duped in a confidence game or dressed in old and/or ill-matched clothes. As a verb, to "guy" meant to mock or make fun of; Austinites regularly "guyed" the "country" men and women who came to town on Saturdays to do their buying and trading. To wit: Two young men from the hill regions above Austin were coming out of a certain fashionable hotel when one remarked, "That was the best cold soup I ever tasted." His companion, better heeled in city life, remarked that it was ice cream. A Bull Creek girl went into a drugstore to buy some taffy-tolu chewing gum (Bull Creek was a rural settlement in the "mountains" above Austin). The clerk, trying to be sociable, remarked to her, "It's a pretty warm day." "You beecher life," she explained, "I heered it was two hundred degrees below zero."

Guy Town was a favorite destination for many of the naïve "country" men who came looking for a good time and often got way more than what they bargained for, leaving "sadder but wiser."

The lights may have shined bright on the evening of May 5, 1881, but less than three months later, responding to a crippling debt problem, the city council ordered many of the streetlamps shut off, including those on Congress Avenue and Pecan Street—Austin's two leading business streets.

"Country Folks." *Author's collection.*

"To have the capital of the state in darkness during sessions of the legislature, is simply a thing which every public-spirited citizen of the city should be ashamed of," the *Statesman* scolded. "Suppose such a state of affairs exists, when the legislature meets next week, and a representative would introduce a bill making an appropriation to supply members of the legislature with lanterns to enable them to find their boarding houses? Will it do to allow the city to remain in darkness during the session of the legislature?"

Coincidentally or not, a few days later the *Statesman* noted that "[c]omplaints are heard nearly every day of promiscuous pistol shooting in the First Ward." The outage inspired wry jokes like this one in April 1882:

> *Julia, there is no moon, will you meet me at the gas light on the corner?*
> *You forget, John, that this is Austin.*

Efforts to bring electric lighting to Austin began as early as January 1882. In December 1882, the *Statesman* whined, "Why does the Capital City not have electric lights? Our sister cities in the state have the light, and it is found as cheap and far superior to gas. The legislature is coming, and it is very necessary to have our streets lighted by some means or other."

In January 1883, the city council had twenty-five gas lamps relit along Pecan Street and Congress Avenue, but by the end of April, the gas company had its gas posts taken down for lack of payment. By November 1883, an electric light company had been formed, and the *Statesman* rejoiced, albeit very prematurely:

> *Soon we are to have electric lamps in Austin,*
> *Flinging their light every way so bright,*
> *Flickering far out into the night;*
> *Lamps that are hung over every street.*
> *Lamps that are hung every other to beat.*
> *Colored and cornered and put up in style,*
> *How they will make the multitude smile!*
> *Lamps that are ever to be seen from afar,*
> *Lamps to be crowned with the bright Texas Star,*
> *Lamps that will move us to mark and admire*
> *The marvelous flick of their delicate fire.*

By January 1884, a handful of progressive Austin businesses had individual electric lights, but by the end of January 1886, there were only about forty electric lights in the city, which was about the full capacity of the plant. And the complaints about inadequate street illumination continued, especially in the light of the "servant girl murders" of 1885 that terrorized the city. From January 2, 1886:

> *In a city of the size and importance of Austin, the almost total darkness which prevails on many of our principal streets is entirely inexcusable. It is a matter that should be brought forcibly before the city fathers and immediate action taken there on the recent crimes which have so lately horrified all lovers of peace and personal safety, that would no doubt have been averted had there been sufficient light to prevent the fiends finding easy hiding places. Their ways are ways of darkness, and an ounce of prevention in matters of this kind, is of much more use to a civilized community than the hanging of murderers. We have yet to catch the criminals before we can apply the remedy.*

By the fall of 1887, electric lines and street lights were being installed throughout Austin, and the *Statesman* was optimistic enough to pronounce on October 14, "Gas, that has ruled and reigned—often with despotic sway—

since the era of the tallow candle, is going, and in a few years will be counted among the obsolete things of earth." And shortly thereafter, the new electric street lamps threw a flood of brilliant rays over the city, including parts of the First Ward. There are only a handful of photos of Guy Town, or even word portraits, such as this one:

Standing under the glare of a great arc light a couple of nights before Christmas 1888 on Cedar street, an officer said to a reporter:

"That's a hard place over there."

"Over where?"

"There, where you see that light," and he pointed to a two-story brick, on the ground floor of which was a saloon. "That is about the hardest place in this city, and it requires constant watching. You had better go over there and take a look at the ranch."

It was a dreary night with a drizzle and heavy mist filling the atmosphere, while the great arc light cast a baleful glare over the entire neighborhood. Very few people were out even in that quarter of the city where humanity, ever restless, tirelessly tramped through the brooding darkness or in maddened revelry battle against it in dive or brothel. No sleep for weary eyes; no comforting rest for weary hearts in that quarter of town when the shades of night gather.

The building to which the reporter was directed was a two-story brick, known in the lingo of the neighborhood as the "Devil's Eyebrow." The name was appropriate, for it arched over and shadowed eyes that saw nothing but iniquity in all its horrid deformity. In front of the building on the sidewalk a group of men and women engaged in conversation in which oaths and slang largely predominated. They gave way as the reporter neared the door, and an ominous hush fell over the crowd. They were sizing up the newcomer to see if there was a chance to rope him in for the drinks.

On the inside the atmosphere was reeking with the fumes of stale beer, whisky, tobacco smoke and the odor from damp and dirty clothing. There was a motley crowd of whites and blacks, men and women, in the bar room, while from a rear apartment there were sounds of many voices. Thither the reporter wended his way, and looking in he saw a hardened crew of bleary eyed men and assertive black and white women of the lowest and most abandoned type. Nearly all were half seas over, and there was a suspicious odor of the fumes of opium permeating the room. They paid no attention to the reporter. In that room the visitor had to make the advances, and woe unto him if he advanced too far.

The room's inmates were scattered here and there, some standing, some sitting, and some leaning against the wall. Some were drinking beer and all had been. The reporter stood by the door and listened to the conversation a few moments. He described it as "incomparable, overwhelmingly horrible. Not a word, not a whisper, not a move that betokened even a faint trace of the higher emotions and feelings that move upon the human heart."

It was hell to him.

The reporter, tired of the scene, passed out of the building and on the sidewalk met two girls coming from a saloon hard by.

"What shall we do?" said one.

"I don't know," said the other, and she ripped out an oath or two.

"We can't let her starve. I won't let her starve. I'm going to take her to my room."

They were talking about a waif from a far away city who had just reached town penniless and sick. In all this city there was no place for such as her. No helping hand save that outstretched by her sisters in iniquity. It was a sad comment on the civilizations of the day.

"Will it always be so?" mused the reporter as he thought of this waif and hundreds and thousands like her, who had nowhere to lay their heads when heart-weary and yearning for a better and a holier life.

The glare of the great arc lights went out on July 1, 1893. The city council had failed to pay its bill to the Electric Light and Water Works Company, and gaslight again shined dimly over the city until May 3, 1895, when the "moonlight towers" that still shine over central Austin today lit up for the first time in a blaze of glory, powered by the electric dynamos of Austin's granite dam across the Colorado River.

When the city clock struck the hour of eight that evening, there was a sudden blinding flash, and the town was in a blaze of white light that hid the rays of the moonlight with its brilliancy. The entire city, from one end to the other, was vividly illuminated, and the streets were as bright as day.

From every section of the city, loud shouts of joy were heard. All up and down the avenue, gentlemen sauntered along, meeting, shaking hands and congratulating one another. Many a "bumper" was drank to the success of the new electric light plant.

It was certainly a glorious sight. For several years, Austin had been groping around in near darkness that threatened the life and safety of all. But that night, the situation was changed, and the change was all made in a trice.

Guy Town by gaslight was history.

CHAPTER 3

1,001 GIRLS AND A GUY

During the years 1880–81, the police arrested about one hundred virtue vendors, as compared with about two dozen from 1876 through 1879. Well more than one thousand *filles de joie* laid back for at least one night's work during the life of Guy Town, and each had a different story to tell—or not.

The girls of Guy Town were a racial, ethnic and socioeconomic rainbow. Some free-lanced, but many more worked for a madam in a sprawling complex that often featured a bar, live music and one or more luxurious parlors, or "sitting rooms."

Prostitution was legal but frowned upon by the "good people" of Austin, despite its utility as a sociosexual pressure valve. Girls could not be arrested for prostitution, but the police found plenty of other ways to rope them in, on charges of vagrancy, drunkenness, indecent exposure, foul language and fighting.

How many prostitutes were in Austin during any year? It's impossible to say; girls wandered in and out every day. Extra girls (mostly from St. Louis, which supplied Austin many other goods) were imported for special occasions, like the legislative sessions, to the point that it became an open joke, like this one in the *Statesman* in February 1883:

> *A very loudly dressed female, very much painted up, of the class that is always very numerous in Austin when the Legislature is in session, put in her appearance at the photographic arena of a local artist.*
>
> *She was accompanied by a young puppy. She stated she wanted a picture of the dog and was told it would cost $2.*

"How much will you charge extra, if I can be in the picture?" she asked.
"There will be no extra charge whatever, I don't charge any more for one than I do for the both of you."

There were various classes of prostitutes: (1) the professional; (2) the secret prostitute, known as such to only a small group of acquaintances; and (3) the occasional prostitute, who would lapse into venal immorality and then resume her regular life. The "professional" class included women in open houses and cribs, as well as streetwalkers who openly solicited in public places and conducted their business in hotels or rooming houses. The clandestine and occasional prostitutes were usually engaged in other occupations and/ or lived at home.

Many "frail ones" were Texas—even Austin—girls, black or white or in between. About 90 percent of the rest came from all over the United States. There were plenty enough Mexicanitas, as well as a handful from Germany and a few other European countries. Two out of three were between eighteen and twenty-five, around 30 percent were over twenty-five and the rest were younger than eighteen.

The average cherie was single. Some were married but lived apart. A few were married (or pretended to be) and lived openly together as such. Some were divorced. Those with assumed names—like Toughy, Chromo, Bull Creek Annie, Buzzard Liz, Cow House Annie, Cocaine Mattie and Red Liz—were hiding their past, sparing their family shame, escaping their family's grip or getting a new start on life.

There aren't many stories about how dollar darlings were enticed to come to Austin, so we go to the definitive national study, *Fighting the Traffic in Young Girls: War on the White Slave Trade* (1910):

> *So many and varied are the ways of procuring girls that it is quite impossible to tell all of them.*
>
> *"Employment agents" sent girls out as house servants to immoral places, to make them inmates. Procurers masqueraded as graphophone agents, as the sons of bankers. A Massachusetts country girl went to a Boston photograph studio where a "photographer" promised to help her find a fine fellow and a possible fine marriage.*
>
> *Villainous men assumed the guise of friends and sometimes talked to the girl's parents about getting her a fine position in a store, and in a number of cases theatrical positions, with large pay. Show business was a strong lure to star-struck teenagers.*

"We use any method to get them," one procurer confessed. "Our business is to land them and we don't care how we do it. If they look easy we tell them of the fine clothes, the diamonds and all the money that they can have. If they are hard to get, we use knock-out drops."

A female procurer canvassed communities on the pretense of selling toilet articles to find girls.

During the summer of 1879, a house of disrepute just east of Guy Town was inveigling young, unsuspecting girls into the meshes of vice under the deception of giving them employment at sewing. One evening, folks saw an old German lady rushing frantically in and out of the yard and of the adjoining premises looking for her daughter, about thirteen years old, who was hidden, in the face of repeated denials, in the house. A well-known young man, who was the main inducement for her to leave her home, was seen leaving the premises. The mother, regardless of denials, maintained her ground. After some time, her daughter came forth, blushing with shame, and went home with her mother.

This was not the first time this had happed, the *Statesman* reported. "Traps have been and are now set to allure girls, daughters of respectable families, into their dens of vice and infamy. The occupants and the young man alluded to should be made to answer to the charge of abduction; and it behooves all parents and brothers in the city to watch well the company their daughters and sisters keep."

Procurers looked for victims in railroad depots and watched trains for young women traveling alone. Country girls were in greater danger than city girls because they were less sophisticated, more trusting and more open to the allurements of predators.

The "white slavers" on the trains coming into the city tried to "cut out" attractive girls—making her acquaintance, gaining her confidence and inducing her to leave the train before reaching the main depot, where the police and the various protective organizations had watchers who could quickly detect a girl in the hands of one of these human beasts of prey.

On the night of March 3, 1879, an Alabama country girl, about sixteen, arrived in Austin on a train en route to her brother's, near Giddings. She had no money or friends. At the depot, she fell in with men intent on her ruin. Incredibly, while they were attempting to deceive the girl by professions of friendship, Ida Lake, one of Guy Town's most toughened cyprians, whose house was just across the way, appeared on the scene, took charge of the girl and gave her shelter and protection until the next morning, when a Mr.

The train station, where Guy Town beckoned. *Author's collection.*

Hutchins offered the girl a home with his family until her brother could be heard from. "The conduct of Ida Lake was noble and womanly," the *Statesman* commented, which were by far its kindest words for her during her notorious career here.

Ida, like so many cyprians, eventually met with cruel fate. On Saturday night, February 20, 1892, Ida was up late and went to bed complaining of being sick. And then, all alone, she died. The next morning, some friends went to her room and found her body. She had been in bad health for some time. Heart disease was supposed to have been the immediate cause of death.

Officer Folwell, while at the depot on the morning of December 3, 1892, noticed twelve-year-old Zoe Clements in company with a white prostitute. He at once took her from the woman. Zoe lived in Elgin, just a short train ride away from Austin. Folwell took her to a reputable boardinghouse. Zoe was obviously a strong-willed girl with a rebellious streak. Was she bent on the horizontal life? Probably not...yet. But anything is possible.

The "fake" marriage was another favorite trick. A young man would make the acquaintance of a handsome girl in Chicago. He was polished and plausible, and the girl's parents, ambitious for their daughter's advancement, were flattered that he should bestow his attentions on her. After a very brief courtship, he proposed marriage. They offered no objections, even when he objected to being married by a clergyman and having a formal wedding. So they went before a justice of the peace who pronounced them man and wife—a fake justice, mind you, who was a confederate of the white slaver. They went at once to San Antonio, where he claimed to hold a very profitable position in a large business concern. When they arrived, the poor girl had her awful awakening, for she was promptly sold into the life of shame without hope of escape from its degrading servitude.

The changing moral times were also blamed for many a girl's downfall, as in this article from the August 4, 1882 *Austin Statesman*:

> *When a young girl gets to be impatient of restraint, and anxious, first and chief of all, to have a "jolly time," she is in a position of at least possible peril. From the jolly girls in certain ranks in society the Jennie Cramers are recruited—girls who mean no harm, but who are so careless of conventionalities that they are in danger before they are aware.* [Jennie Cramer was a beautiful, high-spirited girl from New Haven, Connecticut, popular with the town's young men, whose moral character was considered spotless. She was found dead one morning in 1885, after having spent the night drinking wine with a male admirer and a notorious New York City prostitute. Her death shocked the nation and was never solved.] *Our social customs allow a freedom between the sexes which is wise and healthy, but contains perilous possibilities. There is room at least for the inquiry whether what may be called the callisthenic craze, the cultivation of "mannish" sports, games and forms of physical exercise among girls, may not have been the occasion in part for the diminished gentleness and womanliness observable in the jolly girl of the period.*

Some cheries lay their lives and backs down for expediency's sake. They needed food and a place to stay and had no other alternative. A handsome and well-dressed lady secured lodgings at a well-known house in Guy Town in December 1886. She remained for some days in close quarters, and finally it became known that the lady had become a mother. The lady told the proprietress of the house that she was from San Antonio, and had been married only three months, had deceived her husband and had come to Austin to conceal the evidence of her shame.

"Jolly Girl." *From* Food and Drink: A Pictorial Archive from 19th Century Sources, *Jim Harter, Dover Publications.*

According to *Fighting the Traffic in Young Girls*, "20 percent voluntarily enter such a life, and 80 percent are led into it or are entrapped and sold."

Consider "Pretty Nettie," described in 1871 by someone who had known her in happier times. Several years earlier, had you visited San Antonio and taken a stroll through its suburbs, you would have immediately noticed a neat and cozy residence on one of the quiet streets. Its family was well known throughout the neighborhood, and one of its chief attractions was beautiful, pure and innocent "Sweet Little Nettie."

Nettie was blessed with an affectionate and good mother, and she and her brother were invariable attendants of Sunday school and church. No one ever dreamed that the sacred portals of that home could be invaded by the "destroyer."

But oh!, what changes could be wrought in a few fleeting years. Nettie's mother now moldered in a cold and silent tomb. Her father took to the demon cup and began to neglect her. He no longer sought to render her an ornament in that society she was so well calculated by nature to adorn. He fell gradually from his high estate, until at last he was called to fill a drunkard's grave. Nettie's brother proved himself a good-for-nothing reprobate and steeled his heart against the tears of this poor, brokenhearted girl.

Her cup of anguish was full. She knew not what to do. Bereft of all she held most dear on earth, the future seemed to her dark and fearful. One by one, her lady friends grew colder toward her, until at last she was dropped altogether from society and left alone to battle with the cold charities of the world. The breath of suspicion began to be whispered against her. Report after report to her prejudice went abroad about poor Nettie. With no helping hand, she fell. Shunned by those who had ranked as her equals, even scorned by her inferiors, one morning she cast her frail bark on the turbid sea of prostitution. Her fate was sealed.

One evening, Nettie's old friend saw two ladies approaching on Congress Avenue, well dressed and showing some degree of style and taste. But upon their nearing, he took a closer glance and discovered signs of strong drink plainly marked on their faces. Their sunken cheeks, painted and powdered to bring back a semblance of youth lost to dissipation, and their leaden eyes that gave out almost a vacant stare, furnished unmistakable evidences of their downfall and ruin. Lost to all sense of shame, they took no pains to disguise the pathway they had chosen. But another glance at them startled him.

Could that be Nettie? Yes, it was indeed the once bright-eyed, rosy-cheeked Nettie, whose bewitching smiles had won the hearts of those who knew her in the days of her innocent youth. Poor Nettie; how far she had gone astray. Endowed by nature to wear the crown jewel of her sex, she had thrust aside all, for eternal ruin.

The Victorian curse of "princess on a pedestal" had struck Nettie; how ironic that if you fell, there was often no one to help you back up. A well-placed rumor could ruin you. It is no coincidence that the words "Victorian" and "hypocrisy" go together in our minds like burgers and fries.

There were many variants on the "poor Nettie" story, but then there were the stories like Annie Williams's, who embraced the low life willingly, with gusto and a healthy dose of social rebellion. Sometime in September 1883, Annie Williams ran away from her uncle in San Antonio and started on a life of ill fame. She came to Austin and took rooms at Sallie Daggett's place. On October 1, her aunt came to Austin to take her home. Sitting in the county jail, Annie vowed to never abandon the life on which she had started.

But Annie was a degraded, forlorn and pitiable object by July 1886, nearing the end of life's fitful dream. She had been a good-looking and attractive girl back in the fall of 1883, with many of the attributes that adorned respected womanhood. But since coming to Austin, she had fallen lower and lower until she was forsaken even by her shame sisterhood. She had gotten addicted to the opium habit, pulling in many a hit, until it "dethroned her reason" and she was committed to jail a raving lunatic.

Since there was no "typical" prostitute, their unique life stories would fill several volumes. But the life of Duckie Belcher reads as well as any. Duckie had been boarding with Sallie Daggett as early as 1877, which put her in the pleasuring business at about age eighteen or nineteen.

By the 1880 census, she and police officer John Chenneville were living as wife and husband in a First Ward boardinghouse; there are several references to "Duckie Chenneville." For whatever reason, their relationship was a short one, and she was soon living again at the Maison Daggett. Like her soiled sisters, Duckie was no shrinking violet. Modesty and prostitution mixed like oil and water. Duckie was pulled from the streets on vagrancy charges in April and May 1882.

In early October 1882, a Canadian man went to Sallie Daggett's to have a "little fun with the girls." "Act second" opened with this fun-seeker in court swearing that Duckie had robbed him of sixty-five dollars. Madame Daggett swore that the fellow spent the money and was too drunk to remember anything about it. The court agreed and discharged Duckie. Three weeks later, Sallie, Duckie and Josie Gilbert (of whom you read more about elsewhere) were arrested for disorderly conduct on the streets and each fined five dollars and costs.

Duckie made abusive language complaints at the police station on November 7, 1882, against Emma Hunt and Frank Dunbar (one of Guy Town's "disorderly house" maestros). They had tried hard to coin some new cuss words for the occasion, and this attempt at free trade in words cost them five dollars each. Emma went into the sweet retiracy of her dungeon cell, repeating some of the pretty speeches made about the other woman. Duckie had been fined for the same offense the previous week. "They are all a bad lot," the *Statesman* declared, "and might as well be fined two or three times a day on general principle."

During Christmas week in 1882, Duckie was in court again, charged with stealing thirty dollars from Charles Koch, a traveling man who regularly visited Guy Town. Lacking sufficient evidence, the case was dismissed. On June 24, 1883, and again on June 27, Duckie and Rosa Wilson paid five dollars each for the privilege of being vagrants.

Duckie then left the comforts of Maison Daggett for those of Blanche Dumont's house, where she met her maker on December 27, 1883. The *Statesman* tolled: "Duckie Belcher, one of the frail inmates of Blanche Dumont's house, died yesterday, but not without invoking the prayers of the Methodist minister in behalf of her departing soul in the most earnest manner." As was her custom, Dumont gave Duckie a decent burial in Oakwood Cemetery at her own expense.

Duckie had died of chronic Bright's disease and rests next to several of her kind in a peaceful shaded glade in an unmarked grave, a few yards away from Austin's first millionaire, William Radam, who earned his fortune peddling a quack cure-all called "The Microbe Killer." Duckie enjoyed a first-class passing, or a close to one as a harlot got.

At the other end of death's spectrum was Viola White. Viola White was a waif on the ocean of life, storm-tossed and battered. Whence she came no one knew, but for many months, she had been drifting about in the milieu of the First Ward among the most vile of that district. On the night of November 9, 1891, she drank heavily and, with two bottles of liquor, retired to her room in a small hut facing on Tin Cup Alley. An old black woman found her dead the next morning. Her death was attributed to excess of whiskey and morphine. Nothing was found in her room to indicate who she was. She was another of that class that dropped in a place unknown and whose past life was forever a sealed book. A vagrant of the lowest kind, dying as she did was but in keeping with her life. Buried by the city, her age was listed as thirty-five.

Viola's past life may have been a sealed book, but that was not true of "Pearl Clifford." Dull, leaden skies were overhead on the morning of

Duckie Belcher's grave. *Author's collection.*

December 7, 1888, and it was depressing and gloomy outdoors. It was not half so depressing and gloomy, however, as was the inside of an upstairs room over California Frank's saloon on the corner of Colorado and Fourth Streets, where Dora Wolf, alias "Pearl Clifford," lay stark dead. Her "fellow" had gone back on her, as the "fellow" usually did when his "woman" failed to furnish support. Barely two months earlier, she had tried, unsuccessfully, to rob a countryman of thirty dollars at Mollie Seymour's ranch.

Grief-stricken, she determined to drown her sorrow in the flowing bowls of "bug juice." She commenced the drowning process several days earlier and, becoming unruly, was chucked into the station house. The next night, she was sober, but by midnight, she was "boozy" again, in which condition she went to her room. She had been taking morphine, but since it was a custom with nearly all women of her class, no attention was paid to it. It was also known that she had threatened to take her life, but such threats were so common no attention was given it.

On the morning of the seventh, she came down the stairs, under the influence of liquor and morphine. At about seven o'clock, she went up to her room again and took more of the drug. At about nine o'clock, Julia Alexander, who ran a kind of restaurant near the saloon, found Dora in bed breathing her last. Two empty morphine vials were on a nearby small table.

Dora's family was respectable. Her mother and one brother lived in St. Louis, where her brother was a successful scenic painter for the great theaters. They were not aware of the life Dora was leading. She had been living in Austin about seven years and was described as a woman of more than ordinary intelligence. Her life's history was the oft-repeated tale of woman's confiding nature and man's perfidy. An undertaker from St. Louis reached Austin on the morning of December 11, 1888, for Pearl's remains and conveyed them to St. Louis.

A lucky few girls got a second chance at life, as the *Statesman* reported on February 24, 1882:

Two inmates of a house of common resort in the first ward have lived a life of shame for years past, but at times had indicated a desire to reform, if only the world would receive them. Recently they were given the opportunity of changing their manner of life. A well-known St. Louis merchant agreed to defray their expenses back to their old homes in Missouri and guaranteed they would be received with open arms, if they were really sincere. The two sisters accepted the kind offer, and are now making preparations to accompany him back to St. Louis, and from there they will go to their homes in the interior of the state. Will the world receive them? Or will stiff-necked piety turn the cold shoulder on them, for what they have been? A heart-broken mother, in the declining years of her life, would fain fold the wayward sisters to her bosom and kiss away their sins. She can forget and forgive. Can the world be at least generous and say to them, sin no more?

Their ultimate success or failure was not recorded.

Austin is famous for its "Drag" (Guadalupe Street in the University of Texas area) and drag queens. The first recorded sight of a drag queen in Austin was, naturally, in Guy Town, in November 1874. One Wednesday night, a man was arrested who was attired in clothes of the female sex. He appeared to be Italian or Mexican and spoke broken English; was about five feet, five inches high; and had a dark complexion with very long, brown, bushy hair. He had on a calico dress and waist, a corset, hoops, an immense bustle made of old papers and rags and was as full breasted as a Durham cow, several towels having been used to give him the "swell." Indeed, he had all the paraphernalia of an Austin belle, although he lacked the beauty and attraction to back it up. He was clean-shaven and had a Roman-shaped face, inclined to be a little slender and manifested much temper toward the officers who arrested him, as well as in court the next day. The *Statesman* reported:

Indeed, he seemed to be a villain without tact or judgment—a monstrosity. The great length of his hair indicated that he had deliberately prepared to pass himself off for a woman, [and] a feeling seemed to pervade the immense audience present that he was a house robber. The trial created much merriment, and when the jury brought in a verdict of guilty, and assessed his punishment at $25 and costs, the general expression was that "he got off light." He has been living some time down in "five points." We make this statement to correct the impression that he is not a native monstrosity of the mountain regions of the upper country, and captured by the late exploring and water-surveying party up to Marble Falls.

The "monstrosity" was brought out in the chain gang on November 13, but he refused to work. As a weepist and a poutist, he seemed "to be a successist, but as a workist, he is a total failure, and a fraud on general principle," the *Statesman* observed.

The man still refused to work the next day. "The best thing to do with him is to have his hair cut short and his photograph taken, and then make him leave the city," the *Statesman* pronounced. The "monstrosity" was taken across the river on Saturday afternoon, November 14, and told to leave, but he was seen again that night in Five Points. No further mention was made of him in the papers; perhaps he moved on to more favorable surroundings, like the premium-grade Tenderloin districts in San Antonio or New Orleans.

CHAPTER 4

SUFFER THE LITTLE CHILDREN

Age was not a limiting factor for entry into the world's oldest profession, although it appears to have been no earlier than sometime near puberty. A formal survey of two thousand prostitutes in New York City on the eve of the Civil War indicated that many had entered the trade between the ages of fourteen and sixteen and one or two as early as eleven and twelve.

The age of consent in Texas was fourteen back in the Guy Town era. We know from court records that Henrietta Hardeman, a local girl of color and daughter of Patricia Hardeman, a First Ward washerwoman, was a practicing prostitute by age fourteen. Her rap sheet included theft (she spent her twelfth birthday in jail on her first theft charge), abusive language, profanity, disturbing the peace, drunkenness, assault and battery.

Back in the day, theft of goods amounting to over twenty dollars was a felony and would consign the criminal to the penitentiary. Anything under twenty dollars was a misdemeanor and punished by a fine or imprisonment in the county jail. Oliver Townsend, Austin's "Great American Chicken Thief," knew this and always gauged his thieving accordingly. Henrietta was not as scrupulous as Oliver in observing the twenty-dollar limit, and she paid the price. On October 27, 1890, Henrietta was languishing in the county jail, charged with theft from person of more than twenty dollars. One month later, she was sentenced to five years in the pen.

Maggie Blunt, age fifteen, was arraigned on July 10, 1885, and fined five dollars and costs for being a streetwalker. Maggie was the daughter of old Ephran Blunt, an Austin rag picker, and his wife, Jane, who was young enough to be Ephran's granddaughter.

Shortly after nine o'clock on May 25, 1892, Officer Howell came upon a gang of black streetwalkers—Allie Blunt, Bettie Blunt, Lucy Blunt, Mollie Hancock, Eliza Williams and Mary Johnson—at the corner of Congress Avenue and Fourth Street. The girls at once scattered, but he succeeded in capturing the ringleader, Mary Johnson, fourteen years of age and described as one of the worst characters in the city. (Her first recorded arrest was in August 1891, for vagrancy.) She struggled desperately and succeeded in inflicting a severe wound on the middle knuckle of the officer's forefinger with her teeth before he quelled her. Not having his nippers with him, he turned her over to Officer Bill Davis, who marched her off to the calaboose, disturbing residents all along the line of march with her cries. At the calaboose, she made the night hideous with her noise for fully an hour. The gang of women and girls to which she belonged was one of the worst then infesting our streets, the *Statesman* declared. Nightly they prowled about, their favorite victims being young gentlemen returning from entertainments with their lady friends, whom they insulted, using the vilest and filthiest language imaginable. Time after time, they had been arrested and fined and imprisoned, but it did not deter them in the least from plying their trade. For her troubles, Mary was convicted of vagrancy and fined fifty dollars.

At age fourteen, Mary Johnson was an impressively hard-edged youngster, but she paled in the face of Betty and Alice Blunt. Betty was first arrested for vagrancy, along with Alice and Mary Johnson, in August 1891. Betty was twelve then, possibly just eleven. When Alice Blunt was arrested and convicted of vagrancy in October 1891, it was noted that she was thirteen years old with a ten-month-old baby and that she was already a "frequenter" of the recorder's court.

The Blunt sisters would eventually add robbery to their repertoire. On the evening of March 28, 1895, Betty and Alice enticed J.E. Breed of Blanco County into the alley near the Driskill Hotel and robbed him of $55.00, with Alice going through his pockets. Six days later, Betty spilled the beans to the authorities. She averred that no man aided them but that they carried out the job themselves. She said they had secreted some of the money near the entrance to the yard adjoining DeLaney's Saloon in the First ward, and near the gate post, the officers found $33.75, wrapped in a rag and placed in a hole in the ground. Breed recognized the money as his, and it was turned over to him by Police Chief Jim Lucy. Betty said that his purse was left at her sister's, and she was

"Guytown Playground." *From the* Social Survey of Austin, *issue 15, of* Bulletin of the University of Texas, *issue 273, William Benjamin Hamilton, University of Texas, 1913. Courtesy E.O. Wilson.*

arrested on the morning of April 4, making four people in the city jail suspected of having had something to do with the robbery.

A telegram was received on the night of June 15, 1893, noting that Lena Corbin had died in Waco from the effects of morphine. Lena, described as a beautiful young girl of only about sixteen years of age, had been raised by Mexican Fannie, a well-known chili woman on Fourth Street in Guy Town. Lena's bright, sparkling eyes and smiling face brought to her that lascivious attention that caused her moral downfall, and a few months later, she ran away and went to Waco. Mexican Fannie refused to have anything to do with her body, so the unfortunate girl was laid away in a pauper's grave in the Geyser city.

Considering where they lived and played, is it any wonder that so many "fell"? The most pathetic victim in the history of Guy Town was Pearl Fowler, who by age eight was roaming the streets and bars selling bouquets of flowers at the behest of her mother, the notorious Daisy Fowler. At all hours of the night, Pearl was seen in saloons and houses of ill repute, not going home until the last dive had closed. Everyone spoke of her as a bright, virtuous child above reproach. Rather small for her age, she had light hair, large gray eyes and was hard of hearing.

At about nine o'clock on the evening of October 6, 1885, some unknown fiend coaxed Pearl into the alley adjoining Mollie Seymour's bagnio with the

"Pearl of the Pave." *From* Children: A Pictorial Archive from 19th Century Sources, *Jim Harter, Dover Publications.*

avowed purpose of purchasing a bouquet of flowers from her, whereupon he attempted to throw her to the ground and outrage her person. Pearl began to scream lustily, and a black woman who was nearby ran to Pearl's assistance; the villain escaped in the darkness. Pearl said that the man was white, but she did not know him. The black woman did not recognize him either.

The next morning, a young printer was arrested. Shortly after his arrest, he told a *Statesman* reporter:

> *Last night I went down to Metz' saloon in the first ward. Before entering the saloon I met this child, and she importuned me to buy a bouquet of flowers from her. I told her I had no change, but if she would wait until I went into Metz, I would buy a bouquet from her. I then went into the saloon and had some money changed, and gave her a quarter for a bouquet. Before she left the place I gave her back the bouquet and told her to run off and sell it to someone else. She then went away. After staying at Metz' for some little while, I left. As I got up as far as Californian Joe's, I saw a party in the saloon whom I knew, and I stepped in and began a conversation with him. While I was there, this little girl came into the saloon, and wanted to sell*

a bouquet. I told her I didn't wish to purchase one. She said, "Oh yes, you are the gentleman who bought one from me a while ago." In a few minutes after this, I left the saloon and went home.

I hardly know the child when I see her, and I wouldn't attempt to outrage such a child as that.

Mollie Seymour then told the reporter that some time ago, Pearl's mother asked her, Mrs. Seymour, to take Pearl and adopt her as her own. She was afraid that Pearl, living as she had been since her birth, would, before long, be a girl upon the town, but she thought if she had proper training, she would be brought up respectably. Mrs. Seymour took Pearl to her house for a few days. Mr. Seymour did not approve of it, for obvious reasons.

Pearl's father was Joseph Fowler, a wealthy Bastrop cattleman who was ready for a drink and a fight on all occasions. In 1883, Joe was lynched in New Mexico, accused of having a hand in the murder of two respected citizens. Before his death, he sent for J.P. Fowler, senator from Bastrop County, to come and take his last will and testament. The will mandated that if Daisy Fowler would place Pearl in good hands and let her be raised a respectable, god-fearing, virtuous life, Daisy should inherit a league of land in Bastrop County and about $2,000 in cash.

The will stipulated that Pearl's mother was to release all claims on the girl. When Daisy learned the conditions of the will, she declined to yield to them. She wanted the property placed in her own possession, with her to look after Pearl's education and moral training. As a consequence, the money was divided among Joe Fowler's relations.

Small wonder Joe made the request. Daisy had led quite a life. On the evening of December 21, 1880, Eugene Hall fired into a house of ill repute in "New" Round Rock, some twenty miles north of Austin, with fatal results. Daisy happened to be in the bagnio that night. One of the shots killed Olive Mellville (real name Agnes Lavergne), who was said to be well connected in St. Louis. Daisy was shot, through both breasts, but not fatally. Hall was arrested and tried to escape but failed. His horse was found staked on the edge of town, convenient for skipping. He was refused bail and jailed. A young man named Graham who was with Hall when he did the shooting claimed that he remonstrated with Hall, to no effect. The men left the house a few moments before the shooting, seemingly in good humor with the women. Hall was the son of a reputable widow lady at "Old" Round Rock. Pearl would have been about two at the time. Nothing was said of her.

At the time of Joe's will, Daisy Fowler was a well-known *nymph du pave* in Austin; she had been charged with disturbing the peace and fined five dollars and costs in August 1882. Barely two weeks before Pearl's near outrage, Daisy was again arrested for disturbing the peace, and failing to pay the five-dollar fine, she was locked up.

The young man who was arrested for the alleyway attack on Pearl was arraigned and placed under a $1,000 bond. In his conversation with the *Statesman* reporter, the prisoner said, "[A]s God is my Judge, and as I hope for forgiveness in the other world, I swear to you I am innocent of this charge." The accused was unable to give the bond and was sent back to jail. The grand jury found the evidence against him so slight and indefinite in character that no bill of indictment was found against him, and he was released.

One month later, at about midnight, another *Statesman* reporter, standing with two citizens of Austin at the intersection of Congress Avenue and Pecan, saw little Pearl with her market basket of flowers headed down east Pecan Street. In reply to the reporter's inquiry, one of the gentlemen said, "Yes, she is a midnight flower girl. She goes to all sorts of places, even the lowest dives and most villainous resorts in the city, and almost always in the night time."

"Isn't it a shame that such a thing should be permitted in a civilized, Christian community?" the reporter wrote the next day. "Can a mother be so inhuman as to permit a daughter, a mere babe, to walk the streets at the dead hour of the night, to visit the dens of iniquity that are a black blotch upon the name of the capital city of Texas? Base, indeed, must be the creature who would thus prostitute her child. Is there no law that will protect this little girl, and save her from a fate worse than death?" In answer to his query, no, there was no law.

On June 18, 1886, Pearl, then nine, came to San Antonio in search of an aunt, a dressmaker named Holly. Unable to find her, Pearl went to the Bexar County Jail and slept there for the night. She seemed to be well posted on the world for a child of her years, a San Antonio reporter observed. Pearl's downward slide had evidently begun. By August 1886, Pearl had gone missing. Daisy was desperate to hear of her whereabouts and, if possible, said that she wished to secure a home for Daisy in some good family.

Pearl disappeared from public view for three years, until the evening of July 15, 1889. Three men who ran a shooting gallery opposite San Antonio's Southern hotel were being watched by some men who fancied that they were committing a rape on Pearl, "a new importation from Austin." Pearl, now thirteen years of age, quite pretty and very pert and dressed as a flower girl, readily entered the shooting gallery and went with the men to the back room of the place. That no rape was committed was satisfactorily proved when Officer Bennett arrested two of the men and took them and the girl before Captain Shardein, chief of police. They were released. Pearl was charged with vagrancy and fined ten dollars or twenty days in jail. Although young in years and still wearing short dresses, she had a reputation in San Antonio and in Austin that gave the recorder no regrets in imposing this fine.

Several days later, Chief Shardein told a *San Antonio Light* reporter:

> *I knew her mother for years. She came to San Antonio first with the first variety theatre. That was Daisy Dean's, about 14 years ago. Joe Fowler, a gambler and desperado, was her husband then. Pearl Fowler had not then been born. The old woman has lived in Austin for a number of years and I understand from parties in Austin that she has taught her daughter from early childhood to beg on the streets, and no doubt she has taught her to do worse. Since Pearl has been in jail the old woman has been several times to see her, and wants to get her out. She cannot do so, however, unless she will leave town. They say they will go this afternoon, and I will send a policeman with the girl out to this afternoon's train and see.*

But the *San Antonio Express* reported on July 29, 1889:

> *Little Pearl Fowler, aged 14, seems to be totally depraved. It will be recollected that the police arrested her some time ago for unmentionable conduct in the shooting gallery opposite the Southern Hotel. The recorder fined her twenty days in jail. Her mother came over from Austin and pleaded for her. Captain Shardein's heart softened and on the promise that the girl would be taken back to her home at Austin he released her from the custody of the bat cave. The girl and her mother disappeared for a while, but yesterday the incorrigible youngster appeared on the streets again in the garb of a flower girl, and one of Captain Shardein's men recognizing her, arrested her and put her back in jail. The girl is even more youthful looking than her age would indicate. She is quite pretty with a decidedly innocent appearance. A house of correction would perhaps do her more good than any other influence which could be brought to bear on her.*

Pearl next showed up in the news late in December 1890 as missing again, this time in Fort Worth, where Daisy had sent her at the first of the month to be treated for her partial deafness. Nothing had been heard of her since.

She was then an attractive young teenage girl, and it was feared that some wrong might have befallen her. Two weeks later, Daisy, who was now living a whiskey bottle's throw from Charley Cunio, wrote to the doctor asking if Pearl had arrived safely. She had not, and the doctor inserted a notice in the *Fort Worth Gazette* designed to catch her attention, out of fear that she might have strayed or been enticed away. By December 30, nothing had been heard from her. By November 1891, Pearl was languishing in the Galveston jail on a charge of abusive language. At this point, she dropped out of sight forever, as best as we know, or at least under the name of Pearl Fowler.

Little girls were not the only intended victims. On January 20, 1894, a Mr. Gottig reported to the police that Edward, his eight-year-old boy, had left home at seven o'clock that morning and asked them to keep on the lookout for him. Gottig furnished a description of Edward's clothes, and they began the search.

Edward probably had a very narrow escape from a horrible fate. A few hours after he was reported missing, Joe Mayer noticed him in company with a drunken tramp at Schneider's Saloon in the First Ward. Mayer asked Edward if the tramp was his father. The boy said no and further stated that he was going to San Antonio with the tramp; he did not want to go, but the tramp said he would shoot him if he did not go with him. The tramp violently objected to giving the boy up, and it was only on a threat of violence that he subsided. Mayer took Edward home and the next day turned him over to his father.

A few days earlier, a gang of tramps down by the depot made a small boy beastly drunk and were abusing him in a shameful manner until they were run off by a citizen. The *Statesman* declared that it was high time that something be done to rid the city of the worthless vagabonds.

But the worst outrage of all had occurred in October 1883, when George Wallace, Tom Conley and Francis Lawrie were arrested for an "unnatural crime" upon a little boy, Joe Gibson, whom they caught and thrust into an empty freight car. Then all of these men in turn committed the indecent crime. When they released him, he sought the police and, finding Officer Howe, told him his story. That officer, in company with other policemen, found the men and stowed them in the cooler.

They were tried in district court in December. Lawrie and Conley were convicted of sodomy and sentenced to seven years in the penitentiary. Wallace admitted his guilt; his admission was deemed of more value than would have been his conviction, establishing the truthfulness of the unfortunate boy, according to the *Statesman*, "who, by the way, has so demeaned himself

Top: "In the Cooler." *From* The Rolling Stone, *O. Henry, Doubleday, Page and Company, 1918.*

Left: "Not a Proper Place for Young Girls." *From* The Rolling Stone, *O. Henry, Doubleday, Page and Company, 1918.*

as to receive the confidence and regard of those who have been brought in contact with him. Our information is said he has shown himself to be, while poor and among strangers, a manly, honest little fellow."

It seems incredible, in this time and day, that a little boy so victimized would have to prove his innocence in such a manner, but many children—not just Pearl—were treated as chattel by their own parents. The *Statesman* scolded on September 13, 1893:

> *We regret to be compelled to refer again to the habit of parents of sending their children to the saloons for beer. Yesterday a girl quite 12 years of age was seen to enter and after awhile go out of a beer saloon with a bucket of beer. Permit us again in all kindness to admonish parents that a beer saloon is not a proper place for young girls. However orderly the saloon may be kept there is always danger of their meeting men there who in their cups might teach them lessons blighting their whole lives. Now we know that the love and protection of an offspring is the most natural emotion of a mother or father and if they believed it would injure their children to send them after beer they would rather die than do it. Keep you daughters, at least, free from the contaminating influence of a man half intoxicated, and perhaps half brutish when sober. Go for beer yourself, swig as much as you can hold, and we won't say a word, but for God's sake don't send your children for it. Let us keep them pure as long as we can for temptations strew their pathway all through life, and never let us give them an opportunity to say to us: "You, father, are to blame for my downfall. You loved beer so much you sent me, an innocent girl, to the saloon for it, and there the seeds of my ruin were planted."*

CHAPTER 5

LES MESDAMES DE GUY TOWN

If French is the language of love, in Guy Town it was certainly the language of illicit love: *nymph du pave*, *fille de joie*, *demimonde*, *chere ami*, bordello, brothel, madame, *mesdames*, *maison*, *maison close* and more. Certainly, "*maison close*" sounds much classier than "disorderly house" or "cathouse," as does "*fille de joie*" when compared with "whore" or "cull on the hoof." In France, "madame" may refer to a woman of refinement, but the madams of Guy Town were anything but ladylike.

By the 1880 census, Guy Town was in full bloom, a garden of faded blossoms. Unlike the 1870 and 1875 censuses, madams were now identified by the relatively subtle livelihood title of "Keeping *a* House," as opposed "Keeping House," which is what housewives did. Guy Town's reigning madams during its 1880s heydays were Sallie Daggett, Blanche Dumont, Georgia Fraser, Fannie Kelley and Mollie Seymour.

Blanche was renting a First Ward house with two other women as early as 1870. Fannie was servicing visitors to the First Ward at least as early as December 1872, when the *Austin Statesman* noted that Blanche and Fannie had letters remaining at the post office. Sallie had been lying down on the job since at least 1875. Fannie and Sallie would move on in the 1880s, but Blanche and Georgia remained in Guy Town until the lights went out in 1913.

Their houses were clustered in and around the block formed by Cedar (Fourth), Colorado, Cypress (Third) and Lavaca Streets. "Disorderly" these houses certainly were, as well as the scenes of much turbulence and many a tragedy.

Left: "The Heart of Guy Town." *Map from* Austin, Texas, Illustrated: Famous Capital City of the Lone Star State, *Southwest Publishing Company. Author's collection.*

Below: A1894 Sanborn fire insurance map of Madames' Row.

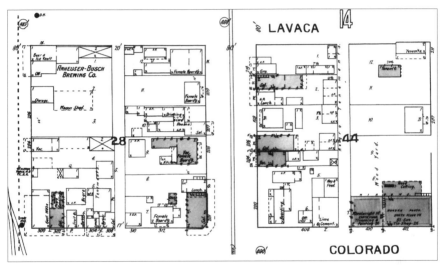

By the time of the 1880 census, one of Sallie Daggett's inmates, Miss Josie Gilbert (nineteen), despite her age, had already buried one babe, a little girl who lived only three hours after birth, prematurely born, in March of the previous year.

Prostitution was legal but frowned upon, and the police did everything they could to could to discourage it, especially harassing the madams, as the following two incidents (out of hundreds) illustrate.

On July 7, 1880, Sally Nicholson, alias "Sallie Daggett" (her putative live-in husband was W.M. Nicholson, twenty-eight years old, who claimed to be a stock raiser), was charged with keeping a disorderly house where songs and loud talking disturbed the peace of others. She was also charged with keeping a house of prostitution. She pleaded guilty to the latter charge and was fined ten dollars and costs.

On July 20, 1880, Sallie Daggett swore out a complaint against William Scott, charging him with assaulting and striking her. He pleaded guilty and was fined five dollars and costs. Then Sally stood up herself, charged with keeping a bawdy house. She pleaded guilty and was booked for five dollars and costs.

A young blood was in from the rural districts in March 1881, determined to make a night of it. He took on a few drinks and proceeded to the classic precincts of Guy Town. He entered Sallie Daggett's and was having no end of fun, but somehow he was not satisfied. Drawing an innocent but exceedingly festive little pistol, he added to the interest of the occasion by firing it off. The police heard the report, hurried to the scene of action and scooped up the young man. He was fined twenty-five dollars plus costs for carrying a pistol, and for firing the gun within the city limits, he was booked for ten dollars plus costs. He promptly paid the fines and left, probably a much wiser man.

About half past ten o'clock on the evening of January 2, 1882, gunshots were heard at Sallie's house. Officer John Watts had been shot, and Emmet McPhail, a cowboy and alleged horse thief about twenty years of age, lay dying, shot through the heart.

Earlier that night, a black man, Ike Johnson, was on his way home from church in a wagon with his wife when two white men on horseback rode up, one on either side, and commenced to whip his horses. He remonstrated with them, whereupon they drew their six-shooters and threatened to kill him. Johnson reported the case to Officer Watts, and the two of them went in search of the men. They traced them to Sallie's place. Watts went in to arrest them, summoning William McClellan to assist him.

The men went to the wine room, which entailed passing out the rear hall door and across a small portico. Watts met the two men on the portico and told them they were under arrest. Without a word, both men drew their pistols. The officer knocked one off the gallery and clinched with the other. The one in the grasp of the officer fired one or maybe two shots, one of the balls striking Watts in the side, inflicting a slight wound. The man knocked off the gallery had recovered himself and was in the act of shooting the officer when Watts shouted to McClellan, who was unarmed, "For God's sake, kill him." McClellan took Watt's pistol from his belt and shot McPhail. McClellan was exonerated for taking McPhail's life.

About half past eleven o'clock, on Sunday night, April 6, 1884, newly ex-policeman Fred Callahan was in Sallie Daggett's house, seated at the piano, when Thomas Bowles, a man named Perkins and another party entered.

Shortly after entering the parlor, Perkins began throwing slurs at Callahan and then asked the question, "Are you down here looking for new names to pull?" Callahan said he was not. After Perkins applied some very opprobrious epithets to Callahan, Callahan got up from the piano and walked over to a table. Perkins again cursed and then struck him. Callahan punched him back. Then Perkins used his knife, cutting Callahan in three different places. Callahan swore that the accusation that he had a knife was wholly without foundation, although he had been several times warned that Perkins "had it in for him" since the arrest and trial of a number of First Ward people for gambling and burglary in which he, Callahan, took such a prominent part.

In 1875, the notorious gambler and pistolero Ben Thompson (who would serve as Austin city marshal from 1880 to 1882) heard that Fannie Kelley had said something offensive about him and went down to see about it. Upon entering the parlor, he proceeded to shoot out the keys of the piano, one after another, with the hired piano player jumping out of the window in such a hurry as to carry the sash with him. After puncturing the mirror and putting out the lights, Ben took his departure. He was not arrested as no complaint was filed.

Fannie was on trial on January 21, 1877, for keeping a house of ill fame. When Officer Sheehan was introduced as a witness, the acting city attorney requested him to state where the house was situated. He replied, "Now what are you asking me such a question as that for? Yerself and every man on that jury know as well as meself where Fannie Kelley's is, and yeve all been thar often."

Madams with a good head for business could lead quite a comfortable life, owning lots of fancy jewelry and houses during a time when married women held very few property rights. In March 1880, Madame Fannie lost a diamond pin containing forty-one diamonds and offered a reward of $300 for its return.

For reasons unknown, Fannie Kelley was living in San Antonio by the summer of 1883, and Blanche Dumont had taken over her Cedar Street rancho. Life in Fannie's new home was as lively as it was in Austin, with shootings, attempted suicides and more. Fannie died in September 1884 during an operation to remove a tumor, which was put on display in the Texas Museum in Losoyo Hall. She left $12,000 in property and money and several thousand more in diamonds and other jewelry. In a dispute over her estate, it came out that she had a grown son with whom she did not get along and that a man named Pratt had been keeping her for thirteen years; she had been sweet on William Kornrumph, though, to whom she gave all her diamonds. The day after her operation, Pratt was at her house going through all the trunks and drawers looking in vain for the jewelry. They cut a deal that left Kornrumph with the house, the lot and the diamonds.

Then there was Mollie Seymour's Cedar Street bagnio and saloon. Tragedy struck Mollie when her son, twenty-year-old Gus Porter, was shot on the evening of November 15, 1878, by two other young men, Steve McKinney and Gentry Bailey, not far from her house of business. A fuss had been brewing for three or four days that resulted in a meeting and an exchange of shots by the three parties. McKinney and Bailey bailed the moment the shooting was done, one on foot and the other on horseback. Porter was shot just below the left nipple, the ball lodging in his back. Porter was described as genial, with a warm heart and manly nature, a popular and creditable student at Austin's Texas Military Institute.

According to the 1880 census taken late in May, three young white doves were boarding with Mollie. But a newspaper account from August 6, 1880, indicated that Mollie was now in Brenham, where at just before midnight on the third, Officer William Garrett was shot three times in the breast and instantly killed by William Allen at Mollie's bawdyhouse. Earlier in the evening, Garrett had arrested half a dozen prostitutes and lodged them in the calaboose. The city marshal released some of them. At about midnight, Garrett returned to Mollie's to rearrest one of the women. Allen was in a side room when one of the girls told him that Garrett had a pistol and would kill him. Garrett, pistol in hand, walked into the room where Allen was. A tussle ensued, during which Allen drew his pistol and administered the three fatal shots.

At some point, Mollie returned to Austin; a paragraph in the March 29, 1885 issue of the *Daily Statesman* so highly offended Mollie that she went in search of the offending reporter, breathing dire threats of vengeance. But as reporters are almost always on the go, she didn't succeed in getting an interview with the object of her wrath until the afternoon of April 1.

At about half past four o'clock, Deputy Sheriff Martin Crenshaw approached the *Statesman*'s city editor and produced a warrant for his arrest. The charge was for "imputing a lack of chastity to a female." It seemed a somewhat strange pretext on which to base a warrant, taking all the facts into consideration, but the reporter went to Justice Thomas Purnell's courtroom. Mollie, her attorney R.H. Brumby and the justice were waiting.

Mollie was armed with a short stick about the size of an ordinary walking cane and was in a rage. Some talk ensued that resulted in the reporter being placed under bond. Suddenly, Mollie approached him and dealt two rapid blows on his shoulder. She kept up the attack, and he had to defend himself as best he could, using no other weapons than those of nature. At this, lawyer Brumby interfered by drawing a six-shooter, cocking it and flourishing it in a threatening manner, evidently with the intention of shooting the reporter. The justice and deputy then interfered, and matters were for a time quieted. The reporter withdrew but was quietly followed by the irate Mollie and again assaulted. She was fined twenty-five dollars and costs for assault. Reports of the event were carried in newspapers across the state.

Mollie had a dance in her barroom on the evening of July 24, 1886, attended by brothers Jerry, Pat and Ed Sheehan. Pat, drunk and boisterous, went through the bar flourishing a knife and cursing everybody present. He first cursed the bartender, calling him all the vile names possible. Every man and woman in the house gave him a wide berth. He passed out of the house, and upon reaching the sidewalk in front of the saloon, he began cursing the cyprian, Ida Lake. Here Jerry interfered and tried to get him to stop and be quiet. This made Pat angrier, and seizing Jerry by the shoulder, he pulled him to the gate leading into the yard. Just as they reached the gate, Sallie Daggett, who was seated not far away, saw Pat stab Jerry in the side, at the same time letting him loose. Jerry exclaimed, "My God! I'm cut" and started east on Cedar Street.

Sallie asked if he was hurt. He made no reply but staggered on, and near the corner of Colorado Street, he fell. Officer Wells and a hackman went to his assistance and, placing him in a hack, conveyed him home, where Dr. W.J. Mathews gave him medical attention. Pat Sheehan, after the cutting, went through the yard to the rear of the saloon and hid until Officer Wells had gone to where Jerry had fallen. Pat subsequently went home, where he was arrested. Jerry recovered.

One of Mollie's inmates, "Dutch Eva," tried to wend her way to cloud land one day in February 1887 with twenty grains of morphine. She went downtown that day to purchase the morphine, and on her way home, she visited Madame Fraser's establishment, where she swallowed the drug. By the prompt and vigorous application of a stomach pump, Drs. Graves and Johnson succeeded in preventing the cloud-climbing act. A quarrel with some chap from Fort Worth had prompted her attempted ascent.

Mollie's house, on Lavaca, between Fourth and Fifth, caught fire early in the morning of February 10, 1888, and although the firemen were almost instantly on the scene, the building was almost entirely destroyed. The inmates managed to escape. It was a two-story frame valued at $2,000; Mollie had been smart enough to have it insured. But it appears to have driven her out of Austin. She does not appear in the city directory again until 1897, when she was out of the business and living in the rear of 210 West Fourth.

There are no surviving photographs of Queen Madame Blanche Dumont's *maison*, but the low life had been quite generous to her. Young Ed Khrohn went to Blanche's compound one day to collect a bill from the Nalle Lumber Company. A maid admitted him into a large, elegantly furnished room with plush carpets, velvet hangings and fine furniture. When Madame Blanche swept into the room, Ed saw an impressive-looking person dressed in silk and lace with diamond rings and expensive jewelry. Arrogant, haughty and unreasonable, she demanded to know what little Ed wanted, and when he told her that he came to collect a bill, she ordered him out of the house, which was fine with Ed; he was scared out of his wits. The bill went unpaid.

But what goes around comes around. Many years afterward, a repulsive-looking woman in a filthy dress came into the lumberyard office and asked for Mr. Nalle. When he appeared at the window, she said, "You don't know me, do you?" Mr. Nalle admitted that he did not recognize her. "I am Blanche Dumont and I want you to give me a quarter!" Nalle gave her the quarter, even though she had never paid the bill for the lumber.

The rumpuses notwithstanding, the madams took pride in seeing that their houses were properly run. "If you want to know who's boss here—Start something," read the signs that hung above the hat racks, according to William Dixon Anderson.

But even Blanche's *maison* had its fits of disorder. On December 7, 1885, Bob Marshan and Walter Morgan engaged in a bloody mêlée in which both were severely cut about the face and head. Marshan was the aggressor. The two men freely used washbowls, pitchers, looking glasses and chairs. Officer Henderson, hearing the racket, hurried to the premises and arrested the men, possibly preventing a murder. Bleeding freely, they were carried to the police station, where they were searched, and a villainous knife with a blade about ten inches long was found concealed in Morgan's shoe. They had a hearing the next morning and received the appropriate punishments.

Two of Blanche's "boarders" died from overdoses within six months of each other in 1894, one being from one of Texas's most prominent families.

In a city that proudly wears its weirdness like a tat on the arm, the weirdest weekend in Austin history was April Fool's Weekend in 1886, the weekend of the "Hookers' Balls":

That Ball.
The Wild Circean Orgies Last Night.

As rumored and as was made known to scores of young men by special invitation cards the public ball announced for the night of March 31 came off. It was given by Georgia Fraser, a Fille de Joie, and mistress of a notorious bagnio of ill repute, and a few days ago she sent out cards of invitation. For the nonce the houses of ill fame in the city were emptied of their evil-minded, unconscionable inmates, and under the protecting wings of the city government, they were permitted to publicly occupy a public hall and engage in wild, dissolute Circean orgies.

A score or more, considerably more, of girls were present, rigged out in all the catching frippery tawdriness, paint and tinsel, peculiar to such women. Some few were in gorgeous attire and sparkling diamonds flashed from numerous hands. To make themselves attractive was the object, and all the wiles and cunning of hell itself were invoked to accomplish this end.

"Was the ball attended?"
"Did anybody go?"
"Were men there whom I know?"
"Yes, they were there."
"Fifty were there."
"Over a hundred were there."
"Alas, it is safe to say that during the night five hundred were there."
"Five hundred."
"Yes, five hundred, from the country, boys from the country attracted by the music and by street reports."
"Strangers were there."
"Scores of well known young men were there dancing with girls in all their silkiness."

The *Statesman* fumed:

For the time, dissoluteness, debauchery, and voluptuous orgies ruled the hour, and all under the protection and by the permission of your city government.

Thus it is under the sanction of your city government are your sons publicly debauched and lured to eternal ruin.

Under the protection of your city government with a police force detailed to do duty at the ball last night, are the lives of your sons marred forever and they hurried on the way to disgrace, and to dishonorable graves. Is it not time to call a halt? Abandoned women and dissolute men cannot be permitted to publicly exhibit themselves. It is a disgrace to the city and dangerous to society.

Eight months earlier, two of Georgia's inmates, Eva Roberts and Minnie Thompson, being in impecunious circumstances and deeply in debt, as was usual with most women who led a life of shame, became despondent and agreed to shuffle off this mortal coil, setting the time at six o'clock in the evening. They procured a quantity of laudanum, and at the appointed time, Eva swallowed one ounce. But Minnie's heart failed her, and she refused to drink, saying that she did not want to die, and immediately informing the other inmates concerning Eva. Eva was fast asleep by the time Dr. Bennett arrived, but he put the stomach pump to use, and by midnight she was cussing just as loud as ever and saying that she intended to make a better job of it next time. It was the third attempt at suicide by "lewd women" in the last two weeks.

Just before midnight on October 29, 1893, Officer Gibson got a phone call that Jim Johnson was terrorizing the inmates of Georgia's resort. He hurried to the place and found that Johnson had run all of the girls out of the parlor and was holding possession thereof with several companions. Gibson told Johnson to consider himself under arrest. Instead of submitting, Johnson jumped on Gibson, punching him in the face. Gibson then drew his pistol, and Johnson made an attempt to secure it. A struggle ensued, with Gibson bringing Johnson to his senses by a blow on the head with his pistol. Thus subdued, Johnson was taken to the calaboose.

The usual quietness of a Sunday night in Austin was badly broken on the evening of September 16, 1894, by a row in Georgia's mansion. The active participants and lookers-on numbered some twenty young men, not a few of them being prominent. The "girls" were having a big time with their many callers. Their gaily colored gowns were to be seen everywhere, and boys were tête-à-tête with the girls in all the parlors, the hall and on the galleries. Beer drinking indulged in to excess soon got the crowd in fine shape, and the fun began in earnest. Jud James called Warren Moore a name that he did not like, and they clinched. Jim Kingsbury became engaged in the general mêlée, cutting Warren pretty badly about the head with a knife. The police's appearance at this time saved further difficulty, but Kingsbury was the only man arrested. Warren's cuts were not dangerous.

On the night following "that ball" given by Georgia in 1886, Guy Town's "Cetaroon" denizens, under a permit from Mayor Robertson, took possession of the hall occupied the night before by Madame Fraser, and "throughout the night, they and scores of colored admirers, and, alas, some white ones, too, danced, guzzled beer, and turned themselves loose in licentious debauchery. If it is necessary for the city to grant permission for such orgies as have disgraced this city for the past two nights, by all means confine them to the premises on which these women live."

The hostess was not named, but there is a good chance it was Laura Hall, who ran "Mahogany Hall," Guy Town's leading whorehouse of "color." Men of all races and ethnicities found Mahogany Hall's menu quite delectable. One of Laura's paramours was Jeff Cain, a white man from a respectable Austin family who grew up to become one of Austin's leading fakirs, of whom you will read elsewhere.

One night in January 1886, Jeff visited one of his best girls, a sojourner at Mahogany Hall, and as he had done before, Jeff adorned the gentle creature with "shady" eyes and other graphic evidences of his "tenderness"; coming to the knowledge of Officers Wilson and Henderson, they sought an interview with Jeff and were about to approach him at Metz's saloon, where he was airing his elegance and good clothes, for Jeff was something of a dude and was always well dressed. Upon catching a glimpse of the guardians of the law and suspecting their design, Jeff offered a race and took the best start. He reached Millett's lumberyard, and with the intention of secreting himself from his pursuers, he threw himself into a puddle of muddy slush that he mistook in the darkness for a dry spot of earth and crawled beneath a pile of lumber. Jeff's good clothes were ruined, and the officers prevailed on him to disclose himself. He seemed tame enough for a time and accompanied the officers quietly as far on the way to the calaboose as the post office, whereupon he again broke away for a race but was quickly overhauled and placed in a cell. He sawed his way out of jail a few days later and made tracks to San Antonio, where he was again captured.

After a few weeks back in jail, he made bond, and later that night, he began to paint Guy Town red. Officer Melungen came along, took the wind out of Jeff's sails and steered him straight to the station house.

Maison mêlées like this would continue to occur into the mid-1890s, when they began to lessen, as that astute observer of Austin's underworld Will Sydney Porter wrote in the August 9, 1894 issue of *The Rolling Stone*, "Bad men are out of date in Austin." And it was understood that the women and the houses were to maintain a relatively low profile.

CHAPTER 6
MIXING THE COLORS

All across the continents,
Everywhere a soul is sent,
A new mix of the races is taking place.
It's what Hitler didn't like
And it makes a pretty sight
—"Mixing the Colors," Iggy Pop, 1993

Mixing the colors—that's what was taking place in Guy Town in its heyday. Rigid segregation laws were only beginning to get a grip on Austin and the rest of Texas.

"Mixing the colors" was a "problem" that extended back to the days of slavery. "A 'very good looking' white lady was seen promenading the streets on Sabbath evenings in early 1857, *accompanied—not attended*—by some of our interesting black demoiselles," an offended writer complained to Austin's *State Gazette*. The lady exhibited such an absence of all pride, such perfect equality, that he could not avoid asking who she was and why she would choose such a companion with whom to promenade publicly the streets of a southern city. She was a domestic in the family of an Austin pastor.

"English, Dutch and Irish servants, who had never been accustomed to the marked distinction of races that existed on this continent, in their ignorance and good nature treated the *niggers* as equals; and the consequence was, the presumption of their black servants had lately become intolerable," he ranted. If you went into a barber's saloon, you were regaled with the

"Mixing the Colors." *From* Food and Drink: A Pictorial Archive from 19th Century Sources, *Jim Harter, Dover Publications.*

latest morsel of scandal by the presiding genius of the establishment. Just the day before at the barber's saloon, the ranter had disgustedly listened to a dialogue between a white man and his barber "in which a white woman's respectability was handled with little ceremony."

The first recorded attempt at interracial marriage in Austin was the sensation of the last week of May 1866, between a white man and a black woman. The affair was to be carried off at the "colored" church, but it wasn't. The would-be groom was summarily dealt with by some comrades belonging to the Sixth Cavalry, who shaved, tarred and besmeared him with filth; placed a placard on his back; tied his hands; marched him through some of Austin's principal streets; and told him to leave.

But the prospect of a white woman marrying a black man was the worst act imaginable. Word spread quickly across Austin on Saturday night, March

5, 1870, that a marriage was about to take place between a black man and a white girl about sixteen years of age. Thinking it doubtful that parents or guardians had given consent to "such an unnatural connection," the city marshal, a reporter and several others proceeded to the place where the nuptials were to be celebrated, where they found the guests assembled ("all colored and at the house of a colored family"), the groom on hand and the bride dressed. They found the young bride-to-be intelligent and ladylike in her manners, although she insisted to the marshal that she was over twenty-one years old. The groom was called on for his license. He produced it at once, and it was genuine but was fatally defective in that it described the bride as a "freed woman." The two were informed that they had better not marry under such a license, and as soon as they were convinced that it was advisable to postpone the matter, the marshal and company retired.

Black men very occasionally visited bordellos run by white women, but white men, on the other hand, frequented black-run bagnios quite often. A disturbance occurred on Sunday evening, May 19, 1872, in a house kept by a woman of color during which a white man named Fletch Bennett ran a black man out of the house with a pistol, bursting three caps at him (though the pistol did not go off). Bennett then followed the man to an adjoining room and shot at him twice. Both balls went through the door, and one took effect in the black man's wrist. No provocation for the attack was ever established. Both parties were arrested and lodged in jail, but the black man was subsequently released.

"Decent" Austinites abhorred all forms of racial intermingling, but white women who consorted with black men outside of marriage were especially reviled, as the following two accounts drawn from the *Statesman* illustrate.

On September 12, 1882, "Mose Swisher, a cantankerous colored individual, is wanted by the officers of Justice Tegener's court for assaulting Charley Pruitt, another vagabond negro. The row was over a low, dirty white woman, who lives down in Mexico and who has been sweethearting to both these negroes."

Fannie Prince, a white woman, and Caesar Kennedy, a black man, were placed in jail charged with living in adultery in July 1885. Fannie had been living in Kennedy's house for some time, taking care of his crippled boy, but others thought that the intimacy between the two had grown too intimate. "A white woman, no matter how low she has fallen, who would thus associate herself with an inferior race, should be dealt with severely by the law," the *Statesman* pronounced.

After the "white folks first" Democrats drove the Republicans from power in Texas in 1874, the state began to crack down on what it saw

Above: "Democrats Ousting Radicals from Office." *From an illustration in* Leslie's Weekly.

Left: "Señorita Bella." *Author's collection.*

as a race problem. It enacted a law providing that an indictment could be brought against "a white person, and…a negro, [who] did knowingly intermarry with each other; or having intermarried did continue to live together as man and wife." Laws and local ordinances against interracial sexual intercourse followed.

Austin's Mexican population first celebrated the anniversary of Mexico's independence in 1873 near the river in the First Ward, featuring a "grande fandango" each night. Quite a number of "Americans" attended both nights, and some of the young men particularly seemed to enjoy themselves, tripping the light fantastic with the "bellas" and señoritas. The *Statesman* advised citizens desiring "tamallas" or "enchaladas" to visit the festivities.

After the celebrations, the *Statesman* noted with surprise, "We were not aware that we had so many Mexican citizens among us, but when Mexico (as that part of the city is called), can support two grand bailes two nights in succession, we can plainly see that our Mexican population is increasing. We understand everything went off quietly and pleasantly."

Mexicans had been largely absent from Austin since the end of October 1854, when most were run out of town by a group of "American" vigilantes on the grounds that "[w]e have among us a Mexican population who continually associate with our slaves, and instill into their minds false notions of freedom, and make them discontented and insubordinate."

Detective Chenneville, on a telegram from San Antonio, arrested Especticion Longorita, age about twenty-one, and Alfreda McBurney, an American girl about sixteen years old, in February 1890. The couple had run away from San Antonio. They were arrested at Charley Cunio's compound, and when carried to the station, the girl wept bitterly. Chenneville telegraphed the girl's parents of the arrests, and her father came over after her and took her to a hotel. He instituted legal proceedings against the Mexican for abduction.

A young white girl named Willie Edwards was tried by jury in Judge Von Rosenberg's court on February 13, 1885, for "vagrancy" and was acquitted. Willie had run away from her parents in San Antonio some weeks earlier, and coming to Austin, she "was run into a low dive of prostitution kept by a mulatto named Fannie Whipple, one of the most abandoned women in Austin." Her parents had come here to take her back home, but being unable to find her, they returned.

As the "black codes" in Texas began to strengthen, interracial relationships suffered, even in Guy Town. The most notable instance in the waning years of Guy Town by gaslight ended in tragedy on the evening of May 25, 1893,

"Mexicans." *From* On a Mexican Mustang through Texas: From the Gulf to the Rio Grande, *Sweet and Knox, Chatto and Windus, Piccadilly, 1884.*

in the Colorado River about two hundred yards below Austin's new dam across the river. The victims were "inmates in about the vilest dens of shame and iniquity to be found in the jungles of the first ward."

A white man, a well-known character about town named Mack Thompson, was living in a camp on the west bank of the river a short distance below the dam. That afternoon, Lillie Carter, white, and "Sour Mash John," a black woman, in company of a "yaller" man named John Walker, went to the camp and spent the afternoon fishing and tanking up on bug juice and other things. Shortly after eight o'clock, the women and Walker entered a small skiff and started to cross the river to come back to town, with the women sitting in the stern and Walker handling the paddle. When in the swift current, the women gave vent to their rising spirits by rocking the boat, which almost instantly overturned. Walker swam ashore, but Lillie and Sour Mash sank beneath the rippling waters to rise no more.

Lillie Carter was twenty-five years old, and her face still retained some traces of her former good looks. Her mother was highly respected in McLennan County, and Lillie grew up in the Christian church. Her father died when Lillie was ten, and two years later, her mother remarried. The stepfather proved to be a monster in human form and endeavored to force young Lillie to yield to his brutal passion and unholy desires. She resisted, however, and at the age of fifteen ran off and married a young man with whom she lived happily for little over a year, until he died. Destitute, she returned home, where her stepfather resumed his importunities. Her only alternative was to accede to his demands or cast herself adrift on the world. She chose the latter course and went to Waco, from which place she traveled from town to town over the state, finally drifting to Austin about five months earlier. Since here, she had been tasting "the deepest depths of degradation, living with negroes of the lowest character and participating in their most revolting debaucheries, as a result of which she has from time to time figured in the police court reports," the *Statesman* informed its readers.

Both girls were buried in paupers' graves at city expense.

CHAPTER 7

AN EVENING WITH VENUS, A LIFETIME WITH MERCURY

The railroad rocked Austin's world, first with the Houston and Texas Central's arrival on Christmas night 1871 and then with the International and Great Northern (IGN) in 1876. Austin summers were as unbearable then as they are now, but the IGN trains brought in fresh foods and goods directly from St. Louis every day: fruits, vegetables, pork spare ribs, ice-cold Budweiser beer, California wines and other delectables previously only dreamed of during the summer months.

These trains also brought hundreds of *filles de joie* to Austin in search of "fresh meat," and there was plenty: farmers and new towns were filling the countryside around Austin, and on Saturdays, these "country folk" came into town to shop and have a little fun. Families went to ice cream parlors. Single men headed for the fancy saloons and gambling rooms on Congress Avenue or down to the jungles of Guy Town, where they could get a girl as well.

The 1875 city census indicated that there were perhaps 15 to 20 active prostitutes in town. Three years after the first IGN train pulled into town, arrest records and newspaper accounts bumped that number up to about 60 to 75. Austin was on a boom by 1880; the population had more than doubled since 1870, to about 11,000 souls, and the number of prostitutes was on a similar rise, reaching anywhere from 100 to 175 (depending on the source) by the time the phrase "Guy Town by Gaslight" first appeared in print. There was plenty of work to go around, especially when the legislature was in session. Extra girls were imported for the occasion, often from St. Louis.

**Will you go in?
Oh, yes! I will go in.**

From The Rolling Stone

From The Rolling Stone, *O. Henry, Doubleday, Page and Company, 1918.*

Getting serviced by a girl, even if it cost a country boy a buck or two, was a welcome change from mounting heifers or ewes in the barn. We know that bestiality was a fairly common country boy practice. One young Bastrop County schmuck was caught *in flagrante delicto* with a heifer cow in 1884 and then tried and convicted of sodomy.

Among the unintended consequences of the Civil War and Reconstruction were advances in the art of pornography for use by lonely soldiers, as well as the spread of prostitution—and thus venereal disease—to thousands of towns and village across the country, including Austin.

With all this widespread sexual activity, venereal disease was running rampant during Victorian America, prompting the saying, "an evening with Venus, a lifetime with Mercury," as mercury was the most popular treatment for syphilis. It deceptively relieved some of the symptoms without curing the disease and extracted its own terrible toll, such as causing you to lose all your hair and teeth.

In cities where prostitution was regulated (it was not in Austin), prostitutes with venereal disease could have their genitals painted with mercury. One of the most widespread venereal diseases of Guy Town's prime was spermatorrhea, defined as the excessive discharge of sperm caused by all kinds of illicit or excessive sexual activity, especially masturbation. Problem is, spermatorrhea is a fictional disease. But the hysteria it caused led to manic depression, insanity, encasing of the penis in an "iron maiden" and even castration.

We know that venereal disease was a common plague during Guy Town's heyday, but we don't have good statistics because of the time's taboos about sex. World War I got people talking about sex for the first time, albeit in a negative sense, the trigger being the rate of venereal disease found in the U.S. Armed Forces.

In August 1918, the Council of National Defense estimated, on a conservative basis, that more than 500,000 adult Texans had some flavor of VD. Texas's state health officer opined that at least 1 million Texans were infected. Keep in mind that according to the 1920 U.S. Census, Texas had 4.66 million citizens of all races, ages and sexual preferences, which means that about half of the adults in Texas had VD, if you wish to believe worst-case estimates.

Newspapers in many cities, including Austin, carried discreetly worded ads for VD cures and physicians (called "clap doctors"). Gut-wrenching guilt and the promise of salvation were at the heart of every product ad aimed at men. Some products and ads were aimed at women as well.

Because condoms were rarely, if ever, used and because there were no other forms of birth control available, pregnancy was always a danger as well. A number of the girls, including Bull Creek Annie Hamilton, bore at least one child during the course of their professional life in Guy Town; often these babies were stillborn or died soon after, from a variety of causes—some diagnosed, such as inanition (starvation), and others undetermined. Knowing why wasn't important; after all, they were the bastard offspring of whores.

But many Guy Town girls chose abortion, whether by a midwife or self-induced. One popular method involved the ingestion of extract of cotton root, chamomile flowers and ergot (a cereal plant fungus that is the basic source of LSD). To avoid suspicion, a girl would visit a different drugstore for each ingredient or enlist a friend to visit the same drugstore at different times.

On Christmas Eve 1886, a *Statesman* reporter was called on to witness a scene that was "sad to the extreme in a negro brothel in the First Ward, where a white woman lay dying. Surrounded by negroes of depraved cast she was stretched upon the bed in a state of half consciousness and was evidently suffering, while the dozen or more women about her kept up a noisy sing of semi-songs that would have been sacred in any place other than where they were sung. The woman was a deprave, has been known to the

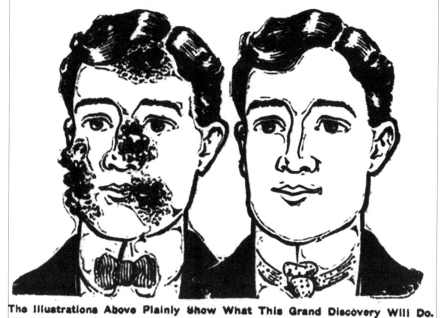

Blood Poison Cured Free

The Remedy is Sent Absolutely Free to Every Man or Woman Sending Name and Address.

The Illustrations Above Plainly Show What This Grand Discovery Will Do.

"A Syphilis Miracle." *Author's collection.*

town for a long while, but she was a white woman, and that she should die in a negro brothel is one of the sad things of latter-day life." Olive Thompson was only twenty years old and died of syphilis; she was buried at city expense in the "strangers' ground." Syphilis is listed in the cemetery records as the cause of death for only a few girls, probably because many of them did not live long enough to reach the final, deadly stage. The other known syphilis victim was in her early forties.

The peculiarities of the marriage relationship in Victorian America meant that thousands and thousands of unlucky husbands brought venereal afflictions home to mommy, who then potentially passed it on to subsequent children. As a wedding present, young grooms often gave their blushing brides the clap or syphilis.

Rich or poor, it did not matter. If you had at least a dollar in your pocket, you could have something of a rocking and rolling good time in Guy Town; three bucks bought you Venus and the Moon. There's nothing in the world more fun than good sex for most men, and since they usually didn't get a rollicking good time at home, given the era's penchants, at least the girls in Guy Town expressed some enthusiasm, whether genuine or feigned. What man doesn't want to be called a stud by the gal he's just "pleasured"? Even if it cost him a few bucks.

"Children" is a key word to describe Victorian-age marital relations; women were meant to be worshipped from a distance. Married couples coupled to create babies, not to have fun. It was "understood" that men possessed carnal desires absent in decent women and therefore were allowed to relieve themselves in the embrace of a lady of the night. It's also the reason that newspapers were filled with ads for devices to help married women relieve their nervous problems, which often derived from horniness.

At the same time that everyone acknowledged the role of whores in accommodating the male population, proper couples had to "keep up appearances." It was another facet of the Victorian hypocrisy of the time. On pleasant Sunday afternoons, the girls would put on their best dresses and prettiest plumed bonnets and make quite a show, strolling Congress Avenue or riding in an elegant hack, greeting faithful customers and tempting new ones.

"It is very unpleasant for a gentleman to be saluted by a *nymph du pave* while he is walking with his wife on the main streets of the city," the *Statesman* noted on October 31, 1882. "It is decidedly awkward and decidedly uncomfortable. These women should not be so bold or else these men should not form the acquaintance of such women. A change is needed in one department or the other."

But not every man cared. During the summer of 1882, the *Statesman* scolded, "White men who ride around the streets at night with common prostitutes should be arrested and made ashamed of themselves—if the latter be possible—by having their names appear in the court proceedings."

So, it was more of a question of who *didn't* go to Guy Town for sexual healing than who *did*.

Ironically, decent folk cruised Guy Town on a regular basis, on their way back and forth to Oak Hill, Dripping Springs and Fredericksburg. There was a convenient place to ford the Colorado River just downstream from the railroad bridge at the western edge of Guy Town.

CHAPTER 8

SISTER'S LITTLE HELPERS

As common as venereal disease was, the numbers did not match the near ubiquity of drug abuse in Guy Town and the rest of Austin. Drug use was perfectly legal; you could buy morphine as easily as a stick of chewing gum. Mothers lulled colicky babies into pain-dulled sleep with morphine-based syrups, the most popular being Mrs. Winslow's Soothing Syrup ("likely to sooth any human or animal"), sold by all druggists at twenty-five cents per bottle. When Little Johnny or Jane had a toothache, a cocaine-based drop numbed things down nicely. And habits acquired young are habits that tend to stick with you.

Cute, colorized advertising cards for the Soothing Syrup and cocaine toothache drops featured beaming children happily at play. Bayer proudly advertised its heroin as well as its famous aspirin. "Patent" medicines dominated the market, but few of them cured anything. If they did anything at all, they masked your pain, thanks to their secret ingredients. There was no "truth in labeling."

Alcohol led the substance-abuse parade. In 1890, per capita alcohol consumption was 13.5 gallons annually, and that did not include the many alcohol-laden patent medicines. Beer was promoted as a family drink, safe and healthy even for the kids. People, especially children, were always dying of diseases caused by contaminated drinking water like typhus. Healthy one day, in the grave a week later. Water could kill you, but beer didn't.

"Intoxication" was by far the most common arrest charge against men. Cowboys, countrymen, doctors, newspaper reporters, professors, policemen

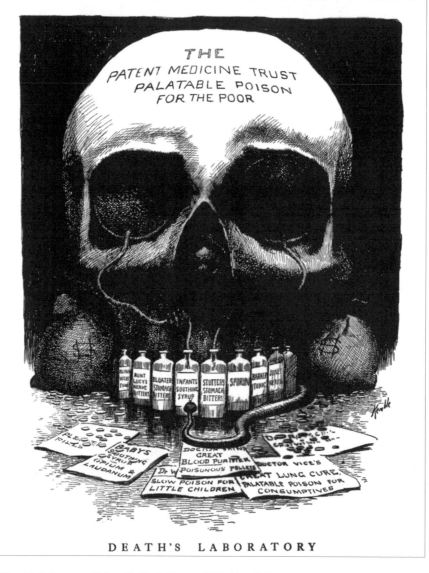

"Death's Laboratory." *From* Collier's National Weekly, *1906.*

"Shuffling Off This Mortal Coil." *From* Harter's Picture Archive for Collage Illustrations, *Jim Harter, Dover Publications.*

and deputy sheriffs all got drunk and were arrested. Intoxication was also the leading cause of arrest for the soiled doves.

Chloroform was the miracle drug of its time, allowing surgery to be more than just a rush against time to cut off an arm or a leg or a breast. With a lightly chloroformed hanky placed strategically near the nostrils, it was "Hello, Mr. Sandman" for insomniac young ladies. For several Austin girls, who fell asleep with the hanky too close, it was, "Hello, St. Peter."

A big belly was a sign of respectability. Only rich people could afford to get fat. The same went for morphine appetites, as the *Statesman* complained on March 1, 1881: "There are parties in this city that take enough morphine in one dose to kill a dozen men, yet they look hale and hearty as boarders who consume that proportion of provisions over their neighbors."

White folks didn't smoke marijuana. Mexican residents probably toked, but it wasn't something the newspapers talked about.

Alcohol and/or other drugs caused the downfall of many prostitutes. Some girls ended up in the profession because they liked being drunk or stoned on something. In 1885, one Austin drugstore sold 718 ounces of morphine, quite a bit when you consider that there are about 438 grains to an ounce and that you could kill yourself with less than 20 grains (about a quarter's worth). Most, if not all, of the working girls were addicted to booze, chloroform, morphine and/or cocaine. Dozens of girls died over the years of either accidental or intentional doses of morphine. Morphine was a cheap and painless way to shuffle off this mortal coil.

Sophronia Johnson, one of the most frequently arrested girls of her type and time, was the first known prostitute suicide, on April 23, 1877. She overdosed on morphine at twenty-two years old. From 1880 to 1895, at least two dozen working girls overdosed on morphine, by accident or by design; at least nine died, but the rest were revived. Newspaper accounts often described the overdoses as suicidal in nature, executed by fallen women grown despondent over their sorry lot in life or from a broken heart. Others just drank themselves to death. Many of them had come to feel world-weary and helpless, that they could not escape their wretched lives. In April 1893, the sitting grand jury looked into Austin's "disorderly houses." Its finding was as follows:

> *We summoned a number of women before us who had the reputation of being prostitutes and living in adultery with different men. From information we obtained we were convinced the majority of them were forced to lead this life of shame on account of having been seduced by some treacherous, demoralized wretch and were harbored in houses of ill repute by so-called keepers as boarders. The board which these unfortunate inmates have to pay these keepers, or landladies as they are sometimes called, runs to the enormous sums of from $15 to $20 a week, which naturally keeps the inmates perpetually indebted to the keepers, forcing such inmates or boarders to continue this life of shame and prostitution until she or they become a total wreck and many of them end their miserable existence by suicide. After careful consideration of the above facts, it is the opinion of the grand jury that the exorbitant weekly board paid by these unfortunate creatures to the keepers is a penalty in itself, and therefore found true bills against the keepers of the disorderly houses only, with the recommendation that the maximum fine be imposed on the keepers.*

This finding was in line with those expressed in *Fighting the Traffic in Young Girls*:

> *One of the greatest weapons to prevent the escape of fresh recruits and to submerge them into hopeless slavery is the system of indebtedness. To break down all hope of escape from the life of shame and bitterness into which she has been entrapped. Nothing has been found so effective as the debtor system. The first thing a girl is compelled to do is to buy an expensive wardrobe at from five to six times its actual value. Stockings costing 75 cents have been charged at $3.00; shoes costing $2.50 are charged at $8.00, and kimonos costing $4.00 are charged at $15.00. The girl was compelled to renew her outfit of finery whenever the keeper so dictated, without regard to her need of it. When a keeper imagined that an inmate is intending to leave the place, a new outfit is forced upon her at absurd figures and she is told that she cannot leave until every*

cent of her indebtedness has been wiped out, and that if she attempts to do so, they will "put the law on her." I have numerous copies of bills rendered against these wretched women in which their costumes reach as high a figure as $1,200 and even $1,500. This indebtedness system is mutually recognized and enforced between the keepers of all houses; no girl can leave one house and enter another unless she is able to show that she leaves no indebtedness behind her.

In one of the recent raids a big Irish girl was taken and held as a witness. She could have put up a fight which few men, no matter how brutal, would care to meet. I asked her why she did not get out of the house. Her answer was: "Get out—I can't. They make us buy the cheapest rags and they are charged against us at fabulous prices; they make us change outfits at intervals of two or three weeks, until we are so deeply in debt that there is no hope of ever getting out from under. Then, to make such matters worse, we seldom get an accounting oftener than once in six months and sometimes ten months or a year will pass between settlements—and when we do get an accounting it is always to find ourselves deeper in debt than before. We've simply got to stick and that's all there is to it."

There were no laws against such forms of servitude or against interstate transport. In the bigger markets, such as Chicago, pleasure resorts had barred windows to further confine their inmates. There appear to have been few if any barred windows in Guy Town, considering the constant newspaper reports of street fights and public promenades and the lack of mention of barred windows in the papers.

Certainly, the humiliation and cost of public arrests did not improve many harlots' attitudes toward life. Even Queen Madame Blanche Dumont was arrested several times for common vagrancy. A significant number of the girls were of the "revolving door" school: drunk or fighting or vagrant on the streets one night, in the can the next day. Many of the white girls paid the fine and costs; the poorer black and Mexican girls usually spent a week or two in jail.

And then there was the ultimate ignominy of the chain gang. A few *demimondes* were put on the street to work on August 11, 1876, for using obscene language in public. But even the *Statesman*, which deplored the excesses of the First Ward almost daily, felt authorities had stepped over the line of decency:

THE HOPELESS WOMEN ON THE CHAIN GANG—A FOUL SHAME AND HORRIBLE CRIME.

The subjection of women, however degraded, to public degradation, is hardly to be tolerated. It is bad enough that these lost and hopeless creatures are shunned by their own sex and abhorred by social law. They are infamous till the very term applied to them makes decency shudder, and when it must be printed only the first and last letter of the damning epithet appears—thus: wh--e! Despite all this, these are women, once as pure and spotless as the best that scorn them. They have hands as delicate and limbs as shapely and brows as fair as the proudest damsel who has never heard a word that would bring a blush to the cheek of modesty. Fallen women they are, and they fell because they were betrayed by someone brutal enough to enjoy the debasing spectacle witnessed yesterday on the streets of the capital, when brawny, clubbed and pistoled policemen stood as masters beside the helpless women to make them toil as guilty slaves in the hot sunlight on the stony streets, and to be stared at by a jeering mob. The spectacle was revolting to common decency, and every gentleman who remembered that his mother and sister are women, shuddered when he contemplated it. They cannot work on the streets; no force or barbarity or exposure to public gaze, and no application of the club or lash can force them to do that of which they are physically incapable, and, therefore, this exposure of women to popular execration must have origin in some personal purpose of which the public is unadvised.

Chain them to a tree. Their hands are small and limbs delicate, and the fetters must fit tightly, and then when these poor creatures, already degraded by the lives they lead and by the oaths to which they constantly listen from men a thousand-fold more brutal than themselves—when these women, starved as they are, and cursed and driven about by heartless men are thoroughly lost to all sense of shame and made to hate man and womankind, then take them back to the wretched dens in which they lead most wretched modes of life and then, when the good deeds of the city government are thus crowned with glory, we may have leisure to reflect that no punishment is inflicted by law which is not designed to reform the sufferer, or others, by the example. In this case a crowd of vulgar boys are only brutalized, and two women, fair enough to look upon, are made whited sepulchers, and the miserable men who must inflict the punishment are degraded in their own eyes. This horrible lesson is one full of degradation to a whole community.

Pressler's Garden

The Austin Pleasure Resort.

South side Pecan street, ½ mile west of Hotel Brunswick,

H. KOPP, PROPRIETOR.

This beautiful Place of resort has recently undergone thorough repairs and is now one of the cosiest and most comfortable resorts in the city. The Garden is arranged with comfortable benches throughout, a fine dance pavilion, and its beautiful groves affording abundance of shade.

PRIVATE OR PICNIC PARTIES

Will find every convenience and comfort afforded them to spend their leisure hours pleasantly. Elegant lunches can be had at all times.

Dancing, Swinging, Croqueting and Games

Of various kinds may be indulged in with perfect quiet and safety from the intrusion of rough or improper characters.

Fresh Beer Always on Draught.

From Morrison & Fourmy's General Directory of the City of Austin, Texas, for 1881–82, Austin. *Courtesy E.O. Wilson.*

"Glittering Promises." *From* Food and Drink: A Pictorial Archive from 19th Century Sources, *Jim Harter, Dover Publications.*

How many of these dozens of denizen overdoses were suicides; how many were accidental? What does it matter? Dead is dead. Let's take a look at a few overdose deaths that also reveal the story of how the victims got to Guy Town.

A young woman known as Willie Summers died from a morphine overdose on October 25, 1881. She was an inmate of a house kept by Katie Franklin at the corner of Cedar and Guadalupe Streets and was discovered at about six o'clock in the morning. In spite of all the physicians could do, she died at half past ten o'clock. As was so often the case, Willie Summers was a *nom du pave*. Her real name was Ellen Leary.

The story of her descent into the low life was typical. About four years earlier, she had asserted that she was drugged by two young Austin men at a celebration held at Pressler's Garden. It was then she was led astray. An outcast from the world, she lived for four long years amid the wild reveling of a career that at last wrung from her crushed heart the piteous wail, "I am tired of this life, I want to die." A few hours after this expression fell from her lips, she took the fatal drug that ended her existence. She was but twenty years of age.

The *Daily Statesman* declared, "The men who led her astray and blighted her young life, and left her to drift out upon the wild, turbulent sea of a dissolute life, will never be punished in this world. Under the peculiar laws of modern society, they never are. It's the poor betrayed girl allured by glittering promises and money—these men had, and now have money—that suffers. The social evil is assuming terrific proportions all over the world, and some law must be passed to check it, and this law must strike with no uncertain touch the men who patronize and encourage the evil."

Annie Miller, on the other hand, was a case study straight out of *Fighting the Traffic in Young Girls: War on the White Slave Trade*. At 2:30 p.m. on Wednesday, February 10, 1892, Annie Miller, a young German girl living over Mrs. Jacoby's eating house on West Fourth street, died from the effects of some kind of poison evidently taken with suicidal intent. At the inquest, Mrs. Jacoby stated that she had known Annie for eight or nine months and that she was about twenty years of age. All day Tuesday, Annie appeared perfectly well, with the exception of a slight headache that grew worse toward night. Mrs. Jacoby had no idea where Annie procured the poison, as it was never kept in the house and the girl had not been out to purchase any all day Tuesday. At about 10:30 a.m. Wednesday morning, Mrs. Jacoby went to Annie's door, which was locked, and was unable to rouse her. She summoned Officer Davis, who got into the room through a window. Davis

"A Variety Dive" *From* Harter's Picture Archive for Collage Illustrations, *Jim Harter, Dover Publications.*

then summoned the doctors, since Annie was still alive, and they worked on her until the time of her death. Annie did not leave a note.

Annie had told Mrs. Jacoby a few days earlier that her parents in Berlin were trying to force her to go home, that Detective Chenneville had seen her in reference to this and that there was a $200 reward for her return. The thought seemed to prey on her mind, and she indulged in a good deal of crying, which apparently led to the rash act.

At her inquest, Officer Davis stated that for a short time after she came to Austin, Annie was an inmate at Jessie Mead's house on Colorado Street. Annie's parents had sent her to an uncle in New York, where she was educated. But "Annie Miller" was really Emma Peech. She was decoyed away from her uncle's home and taken to a variety dive in Houston. While on the steamer coming to Houston, she was seduced, and to avoid detection, she shaved her head and came to Austin. Chenneville received information as to her absence from New York, located her and identified her by a picture. She confessed to him that she was the right party and expressed a willingness to go home if she could conceal her shame from her parents. Evidently, she changed her mind.

After several years of determined resistance, Austin got its first opium den sometime during the first few months of 1884. Not that smoking opium was illegal. By the summer of 1885, there were hundreds of opium smokers in Austin, men and women. The average citizen imagined that they belonged exclusively to the lower and depraved classes. A *Statesman* reporter set out one night to disabuse the public mind of this error:

> *"Where are these joints?" asks the public.*
>
> *The Statesman replies, Search for them and you cannot miss them. There are no flaming advertisements to attract the wayfarer, no sign board to direct his steps. He must search, and probably he will stumble upon some dingy house, with closed shutters, and a stillness of death reigning around the premises.*
>
> *The reporter was wandering over the city in the dead hours of the night when his attention was directed across the street by seeing a closely veiled woman rap upon the door of a low frame house, in a particular manner. The reporter stepped back in the shadow just as the door opened, admitting a faint glimmer of light. Something in a low tone passed between the man and veiled figure, then the woman stepped over the threshold, and the door creaked and closed upon its rusty hinges.*
>
> *The peculiarity of the movements excited in the reporter's mind, suspicion of something wrong. He crossed the street and stopping at the door the woman had entered, placed his ear to the panels and listened. All was still. He moved cautiously around the house, listening at every step. Suddenly he heard a step and stepped into the shadow.*
>
> *Once more the door was opened to admit a female closely veiled. As the door opened, the veil was raised, disclosing a face pale, but beautiful. The beautiful mouth twitched nervously. An expression of pain rested upon that beautiful face, the eyes were heavy, and the body was in a listless attitude.*
>
> *"The opium smoker!" ejaculated the reporter softly to himself. She stood for a moment only, then glided into the precincts of the horrid den, and the door closed once more.*
>
> *The reporter rolled a barrel up to a window and got on the top, for a good view of the interior. On couches in different points in the room laid, perhaps, a half-dozen women, all with long pipes in their mouths. The room was filled with smoke, almost blotting out the one dingy lamp which swung from the low ceiling. What a cheerless room, and what a scene! The Statesman reporter gazed upon this scene for some time, but at last he began to feel drowsy from the effects of the smoke which ensued from the room, and he stepped down and vacated the premises in short order. These dens were*

"An Opium Den." *From* Harter's Picture Archive for Collage Illustrations, *Jim Harter,* *Dover Publications.*

visited every day and night, night customers being the best, they, as a general *saying, being people who bear good names, and they paid higher prices for* *the pleasure of the pipe and the secrecy.*

Syringes and such were common household items in Austin homes by the Gay Nineties, for injecting morphine or those two exciting newcomers heroin and cocaine—or perhaps, in reverse fashion, for cleaning out your diseased urethra or vagina. The syringe was the star player in Guy Town's "Queen" overdose, which took place on the afternoon of September 18, 1891.

Mary Jane Walsh was the colored mistress of a bagnio at 305 West Second Street, and one of her brightest household ornaments had been Marie Bernard, a voluptuous twenty-six-year-old, cream-colored creole recently arrived from New Orleans and then going by the name Marie Loeb. She was unusually bright and was a great favorite among "the girls," but she had recently been cultivating a love for the soothing effects of morphine, which her friend, Ida Stotts, had been injecting into her arm. Ida's mother was Lottie Stotts, who had a morphine problem of her own.

Earlier that morning, Marie was fined ten dollars for disturbing the peace, and that afternoon, in company with Minnie Lee Washington, she started to the bathhouse. En route, they stopped at Ida's house, and she politely gave Marie a shot of morphine in her left bicep. She had already taken a dose or two before she reached Ida, and it was asserted that she stole Ida's bottle and gulped down the contents.

Marie and Minnie proceeded on their way to the bathhouse, arriving there shortly after two o'clock. Almost immediately, Marie complained of feeling unwell and reclined on a couch in the bath keeper's quarters. She was still lively and talked in a jolly manner with Minnie, but she soon became drowsy and lay down to sleep. She never awoke, despite medical assistance, and died shortly after four o'clock. Ida Stotts was promptly arrested but then released. Marie was buried the next day by the city, as was so often the case with the deceased doves of Guy Town.

One week later, Ida was in the Travis County Jail on a charge of assault with intent to kill and murder in San Antonio. On the morning of her arrest and incarceration, she became violently ill and sent for the jailer, declaring that unless she had a doctor she would die at once. When Dr. Graves arrived, he found Ida lying on her face on the cell floor. She was in the throes of withdrawal. Graves gave her a prescription, and she was escorted to the county jail in San Antonio.

As has been the case with so many fashion trends, cocaine abuse started among the high society of New York City in the 1880s and was a favorite among Austin drug addicts by the 1890s. In March 1894, Officer Gibson arrested Emma Tweedle one day for disturbing the peace. When chock-full of cocaine, or coming down off it, she was really dangerous when she got on the warpath. Emma had gotten up that day in a bad humor, and by the time she got out in the street, she was in a very irritable humor.

Among the first things she did was sidle up to a white man standing on the curbstone and plunk him off into the gutter. She proceeded on up the street, never stopping a moment to think, and jumped Officer Gibson, who asked fair Emma what she meant. She immediately told him to go down under the earth and find out and so on. On the way to the police station, the fair lady fought like a tiger. When she was within a block of the station, she picked up a rock with the evident intention of hitting Gibson. He forestalled her, however, took the rock away from her and cracked her over the head instead. It was well for Officer Gibson to exercise care to prevent injury to himself. Emma had beaten his ribs black and blue about a year earlier with a rock under similar circumstances.

Cocaine abuse had gotten so bad outside Guy Town proper that Porter's *Rolling Stone* noted in June 1894 that West Seventh Street, from Congress Avenue westward one block, was infested each night with the lowest, most disreputable and depraved characters of the "gentle sex," who were keeping the cocaine route well traveled. It was almost impossible for a lady to travel in this locality after dark, even with an escort, on account of the impudent behavior of these street nuisances.

Prostitutes obviously did not die just from drug overdoses. While drunkenness is cited as the cause of death in several cases, the various ravages associated with alcoholism no doubt killed many of these women. By 1900, the average life expectancy of the American woman was forty-eight years. Guy Town gals were lucky to get past thirty.

It's hard to get a good grip on the total number of annual deaths among practitioners of the oldest trade, but we can get some idea from newspaper accounts and, to a lesser degree, from cemetery records, based on age at death, marital status, where and by whom they were buried, notes about how long they had lived in the city and the cause of death. For instance, a single woman who had come to Austin from another state or country only a few weeks or months earlier, and who was buried in the strangers' ground by the city or county, was probably a prostitute or a servant girl. During the height of Guy Town's notoriety, two to three dozen deaths fitting this profile happened in Austin each year, so let's say about a dozen to a dozen and a half of them were whores. Even during Guy Town's final years, it's relatively reasonable to assume that the death rate among prostitutes was between five and ten per year, although this guess is even less precise since Oakwood burial records by this point often neglected to give the deceased's age, cause of death or even burial plot. But there was a dramatic drop-off of deaths among twentysomething women beginning in 1914, the year after Guy Town closed.

CHAPTER 9
FAKIR, TAKER

G uy Town brimmed over not only with whorehouses and saloons but also with confidence men and their dupes. Gambling was legal in those days, and honest gamblers were regarded with some respect. Plenty of games in Austin were conducted "on the square," with no attempt made to defraud the players. The proprietors of these establishments maintained a fair game, for the reputation of their houses were at stake.

Fakirs were a different breed. A few days after the name "Guy Town" first appeared in print (March 16, 1880), the *Statesman* warned, "There is a certain quarter of this blessed city where the fashionable seraglio and low bagnios flourish. Here the well-dressed 'fakirs' spread their meshes and cog the dice and calmly take in the unwary. They browse about the neighborhood pretending to be stupidly drunk at unseemly hours, and woe be unto those who are not up to city ways and doings. The fakirs are there for the sole purpose of pulling the wool over the eyes of the young man from the country and many are they that are gobbled up and fleeced of all they have."

The fakirs worked various scams, and they roped in some verdant fellow almost every day. When they noted the arrival of a "countryman" and ascertained that he had a roll of bills, a "capper" (or decoy) would walk up and greet him as an old friend. The man from the rural districts wouldn't remember having seen the capper before, but the other seemed to know him and was so very friendly that soon they were drinking together and chatting away like old friends. At night, the countryman would take his leave to take a look at the city.

"A Square Game." *From "Out West on the Overland Train,"* Leslie's Magazine, *Frank Leslie, 1877.*

By chance in some bar, perhaps, he would meet his entertaining friend again, and the two would stroll down to Guy Town. Here they would meet with some very gay gentlemen—and ladies too—and after some beer or wine, one of the jolly crowd would propose a game of cards. The rustic would usually object at that point. He was not an entire idiot, and he had heard how men had, under like circumstances, parted with their wealth. He remembered that he had with him, snugly hidden away in an inner pocket, anywhere from $1 to $200. The fakirs were aware that he had

"A Well-Dressed Fakir." *From* On a Mexican Mustang through Texas: From the Gulf to the Rio Grande, *Sweet and Knox, Chatto and Windus, Piccadilly, 1884.*

it, too, and they meant to secure the "boodle." Even though the rustic would object at the start, his first acquaintance would assure him that they didn't care to play for money, only for the drinks, and propose to go partners with his country friend. All the others would urge him on, and he would yield. This was the opening wedge.

The countryman and his sleek partner would win the beer nearly every time, until former got so full that he was willing to put up a dollar, maybe, and again they were successful. Per chance the game was euchre, and while the others cursed their ill luck, the countryman and his "pard" raked in the coin. Presently the capper's friend, who was dealing and was one of the losers, after having thrown out three cards all around, stopped and looked at his own hand. He would remark, "I wish this was poker we were playing, and I think our luck would change." All of them then would examine their hands. The fellow they were roping in was rather astonished to see that he held three aces, which his partner assured him was sure to win every time. They generally managed to get the "sucker" to put up his last cent, and then they all threw down their hands. The gentleman who dealt or his partner would show up a "flush"—that is, three of any other suit—which, with a singular unanimity of opinion, they all declared beat three aces.

What if the guy had little more than pocket change? No problem. His horse would do nicely. After the guy bet at poker, and of course lost, the fakirs, astonished beyond measure and with a generosity unparalleled in the history of their ilk, felt sorry for him and offered to buy his horse and pay double his value. The young man, astonished, felt happy at his good luck and ordered drinks for all, as well as accepted the offer for his horse. The affable

"Not So Stupidly Drunk." *From Sketches from* Texas Siftings, *Sweet and Knox, S.W. Green's Son, 1882.*

fakirs then drew a draft on the First National Bank for the amount and, with a sérénité of demeanor truly sublime, handed it to the young man.

They then asked him to take a nip, sit down and try another hand at euchre. Their ways were so exceedingly childlike and bland that the man consented, and soon he had another marvelous poker hand. Betting was again in order, but alas, he had no money—nothing but the check for his horse. Just then, one of the generous fakirs kindly offered to cash his check and go halves with him. The man accepted and lost, and the fakirs, having all of his money, his horse and the check, had no more use for him, and he being comfortably drunk by this time, was rolled in the gutter to snooze the hours away.

What could the greenhorn do the next morning? Nothing. There was no law to make the conspirators disgorge, nothing making such villainy a felony. The better class of gamblers lent no encouragement to these schemes of robbery.

One of the fakir's essential tools was the "spiel piece." Since they spent as freely as they took, fakirs often found themselves dead broke, whereupon it was time to find another "sucker" and play for money again. They would pull out one or more spiel pieces. Spiel pieces came in three or four different sizes, manufactured in Chicago from brass or copper and imitated, as near as possible, genuine $2.50, $5.00, $10.00 and $20.00 gold pieces. They were worth about one cent apiece and imitated the genuine coin just enough to keep within the confines of the law against counterfeiting. They were not bright, and when they were put up as genuine money, the victim, who was generally half drunk and bleary-eyed, believed they were.

"The young man from the country is warned to beware of the fakirs and their raffles, their numbered cards, their show business, and their spiel marks. When they haul out these, their object is to rob you," the *Statesman* warned.

"Trotters," another popular swindling game, was a three-card trick in which the victim was dealt three aces, apparently so strong a hand that he was sure to bet on it. That was the game into which Charles Cook and Jeff Cain steered Henry Glyfe in August 1885. Henry was a foreigner and utterly unacquainted with written English. After several games that led to treats at Glyfe's expense, the sharps induced him to write his name on the bottom of a sheet of paper, and above the signature they wrote a bill of sale conveying to them Glyfe's horse and buggy. When the unhappy foreigner became aware of the nature of their designs, he refused to give possession, whereupon Cain and Cook proceeded to obtain it *vi et armis*. Fortunately for Glyfe, a few vigilant officers halted it in the midst of the consummation.

Besides Jeff Cain, Austin's most notorious fakirs were the Burlage brothers, Chip, Joe and Alf, who despite an honorable upbringing were as free from morals as baby Jesus was from sin.

Usually the only thing lost in these confidence games was the countryman's poke, but in one scam, twenty-one-year-old James Simms

See him do it.
Can John find the ball?
Is it in the cup?
No, it is not in it:
Neither is John.

From The Rolling Stone

"See Him Do It." *From* The Rolling Stone, *O. Henry, Doubleday, Page and Company, 1918.*

Jr., son of the prominent Austin stonemason and police officer who had led one of the early fights to shut down Guy Town, was shot dead, in the predawn hours of March 10, 1880, just three days before the name "Guy Town" debuted in print.

It was a wet, cold night, tailor-made for some healthy drinking. Earlier that night, young Simms, Chip Burlage and another "sport" named Red Ryan determined to have a little fun. Burlage met up with Simms at the Casino variety theater, where Simms was working. After meeting Ryan, they went down to visit Sallie Daggett's and then Blanche Dumont's bordellos, where they stayed for some time before wandering over toward the Gem Saloon (present-day Fourth and Lavaca), Guy Town's most notorious watering hole. They had been drinking considerably and, along about the wee sma' hours, were half seas over and having a time of it. About half past four o'clock in the morning, they ran into "Frenchy" Shubert—a former Blanco County deputy sheriff—fresh in town from Blanco and an entire stranger to them. Shubert, who had also been drinking, was in the company of Lizzie Black, one of Guy Town's most notorious women of the night, who kept a modest house of ill repute next door to the Gem.

According to Shubert, the three young men stepped up to him in the dark and asked if he could change a dollar. He felt in his pockets and informed them that he could not, as he had nothing less than a dollar himself. They then invited Shubert to go to the Gem Saloon and take a drink, remarking that they could get their dollar changed there. He and Lizzie went with them, and when they entered the saloon, the trio proposed to play a game of euchre for the drinks, but Shubert refused to play. They then said that if Shubert would join the game, they would pay for the drinks if he lost. Shubert sat down, and they commenced to play. After playing a short time, Shubert said that he got three aces, and they proposed to turn the game into poker and bet on their hands. Shubert said that he refused to bet.

Then, according to Shubert, they jumped up, and one of them struck him a terrible blow on the head with what he thought was a pair of brass knuckles. The blow stunned him considerably, and while two of them kept hold of him and struck him in the face and over the head, the third one was trying to get his hands into Shubert's pockets. Shubert drew his pistol as rapidly as possible, as Simms shouted, "Look out boys, he's got a gun." He fired at random across his breast to the left and then shot to the right. At the first shot, Simms fell, and the others fled. As they were strangers to him and were attempting to rob him, Shubert figured that they would try to kill him. He said that he had several ten-dollar bills and nine dollars in silver in his pockets. They knew he had it, for they saw it when he drew it out to look for change for them. They got all the money he had during the scuffle except three dollars.

After the shooting, Shubert walked back to his wagon and waited to give himself up to the proper officers. Burlage and Ryan countered in court that Shubert, feeling aggrieved at the turn the game had taken after Burlage dropped a spiel piece on the table and proposed that the game be changed from euchre to poker, pulled a pistol and fired two shots.

Shubert bore unmistakable evidence of bad usage. He had a large knot on the left side of his head and a large bruised place under his left eye, while his face bore severe scratches. The ball fired at Simms lodged against the boy's spinal column, and he died the next evening. The second shot passed through both lapels of Ryan's coat, knocking off the top button of his vest,

S. K. MORLEY,   W. J. MORLEY,

Morley Brothers,

WHOLESALE and RETAIL DEALERS IN,

Pure Drugs, Medicines, Chemicals,

Toilet and Fancy Articles,

No. 203 East Pecan Street,

AUSTIN,   TEXAS.

Above: *From* Morrison & Fourmy's General Directory of the City of Austin, Texas, for 1881–82, Austin. *Courtesy E.O. Wilson.*

Left: Morley's drugstore. *Author's collection.*

and ranged within two or three inches of his heart but caused no corporal damage. The grand jury failed to find a true bill against Shubert for killing young Simms.

Chip Burlage's impressive arrest record included assault, malicious mischief, gambling, carrying illegal weapons, disturbing the peace, vagrancy, intoxication and more. Despite his dubious record, Chip (a painter by trade) had lots of loyal friends in Austin and served for a number of years as a fireman with Hope Hook and Ladder Company No. 2, alongside City Marshal Ben Thompson and Detective John Chenneville, who spent as much time running Chip into the clink as they did fighting fires with him. Chip died in January 1889 of pneumonia; he was thirty-one years old.

Brother Joe Burlage tried more sophisticated cons. Late one night in May 1880, Joe, well dressed and affable, accosted an innocent-looking gent from Round Rock, intent on comfortably steering him in to a kiosk adjoining Morley's drugstore.

"You are from the country, I believe," said the cheerful Joe.

"Yes, I'm from Round Rock," said the countryman.

"Ah, you are the very man I want," said Joe. "I'm in the show business and want 500 bills posted up in Round Rock and Georgetown. I would like 150 of them billed in Round Rock and the balance in Georgetown. Can you do the work for me?"

"Yes, I think I can if you pay me."

"Very well, we will step into my office, and I'll see about getting the bills." When inside, Joe innocently began to shuffle a lot of numbered cards. "These are raffling cards," he kindly explained. "I'm also in that business, and had you been here half an hour ago, you could have made money. You see, there are five cards here, and I would have posted you so you could have certainly won a fine gold watch, and I would have bought it from you. Here are five cards, and you being posted, would have skillfully tried them until you got hold of one that would not easily slip from my fingers. This is always the winning card."

Just as this explanation was made, strange to say, in stepped another well-dressed stranger, who bet Joe cigars that he could guess the winning hand. Joe slyly winked at the countryman as the well-dressed gent drew a card. He won, of course, and bet several times, always successfully and appearing greatly elated. He turned to the countryman and said, "I'll bet you two-fifty or five dollars that you can't draw the right card."

The wily Joe at once brightened up and cast innumerable sly winks at the man from Round Rock, as much as to say, "Now's your time—remember the card that will not slip easily." But the countryman wouldn't buy it. Placing his thumb on the end of his nose and extending his fingers, he gave them a few impressive wiggles and calmly glided out the door.

Burlage and his fakir friend were disgusted and repaired to the back room, where they licked their wounds and renounced show business forever. Three weeks later, Joe Burlage had jumped town; there were thirteen indictments against him. Joe and Miss Alice Raven went down to San Antonio and got married in March 1884. Marriage did not chasten Joe. In the next year, he was arrested for shooting up the town, swindling, assault and street fighting before dying of acute dysentery. He was twenty-eight years old.

But the most fetid of this unsavory trio of brothers was Alf Burlage. In August 1885, he tried to scam his own sister, Mrs. L.E. "Kate" Edwards. Sister Kate received a telegram from San Antonio early in the afternoon of August 20, stating, "Laura is dead. Send $75 for her remains. Georgie and mother will come with the body. Send money to S.B. Wilcox, number 210 East Commerce street. J.W. McKnight."

The telegram was handed to Mrs. Edwards while she was in the post office. The shock to her was terrible, and she came near fainting. Colonel DeGress came to her aid, assisted her into a carriage and sent her home. Mr. Charles Anderson, of the real estate firm of Maddox Bros. and Anderson, promptly sent seventy-five dollars by telegraph to the place designated in the telegram.

Three hours later, Anderson telephoned to San Antonio to a friend to learn the particulars of the child's death. Imagine his astonishment when the news came back that Laura was then at the home of a family friend, alive and well. Anderson then telephoned to have the payment of the seventy-five dollars stopped, but he was too late; the money had been paid, and the man receiving it had disappeared. Anderson then telephoned to have Laura kept from the streets and to let no one see her under any pretense. He also telephoned the San Antonio police to leave no stone unturned to capture Alf.

At 5:00 p.m., Mrs. Edwards received a telegram from San Antonio: "Sister—Laura is well. I received the money. Will be in Austin tomorrow. Alf. Burlage." Anderson telephoned at once to have Burlage arrested, and then he and Mrs. Edwards left for San Antonio to investigate the matter. They returned on August 22 from San Antonio with young Laura. Alf was on the lam.

Wilcox, who received the seventy-five dollars, proved to be a disinterested party. He had met Burlage a few days before, and on the day in question, Burlage went to him and told him that the child was dead and that Mrs. Edwards would send him seventy-five dollars to pay burial expenses. When the money arrived, Burlage went to see Wilcox, who refused to pay him the money without a proper receipt. Burlage gave the proper receipt, and Wilcox gave the money to him. McKnight, whose name was signed to the telegram, knew nothing, having been absent from the city at the time.

Alf took the train from San Antonio to Houston, where he was seen disembarking at the station. He disappeared into the maw of the Houston underworld. Soon the whole police force was scouring the city for Alf. He was seen entering one gambling house and then another. Hearing that he had gone to visit some house of prostitution, they took in every house of the kind but failed to find Alf.

A few deputies were at the depot watching the outgoing trains for Alf. They watched several trains without success, and acting on intuition, they took the train to Austin as far as Cheney junction. Just as the train came to a halt, a man standing on the platform asked one of the deputies, who was standing on the steps of the car, to assist him into the train. It was Alf. A hack driver had driven him out to Cheney junction. The deputy told him no, but said that he would assist him back to town, where he was a wanted man. Alf protested but then said, "Yes, I got that money. What are you going to do about it? Where are your papers?" The officers ignored him and waltzed him into town to await deportation to San Antonio.

Upon his arrival at the Houston jail, he asked the jailer if there was not a place there for a gentleman. "If there is, I would like to be placed in it, as quarters among the thieves and robbers is very objectionable to me." Jailer Paris informed him that the rooms for gentleman were all taken and that he would have to make the best of it in the common cells.

Mrs. Edwards, incredibly, said that she would not say a word against her brother if it came to a trial. Despite her support, Alf was convicted of forgery and sentenced to three years in the state penitentiary. By 1901, Alf was a peddler, living in Guy Town. Alf died in September 1910.

There were plenty of other opportunities for trickery. In the spring of 1883, parties were buying up the newly issued "Liberty" nickels. As they were minted without the word "cents" on them, with only a large Roman *V* to indicate the denomination, they were being gilded or washed with gold and passed on to the unwary as five-dollar gold pieces. "Remember that every real five dollars in gold has this inscription under the eagle: 'Five dol.,'" the *Statesman* warned.

By 1883, the criminal element was so well established in Austin that the *Statesman* felt compelled to explain some of the "Jargon of Thieves":

"Ready for the Kill." *From* Food and Drink: A Pictorial Archive from 19th Century Sources, *Jim Harter, Dover Publications.*

A man must be pretty well posted to understand the drift of what has become the current vernacular of the hardened criminals and "bad citizens."

The word "cat" is often used as an adjective as a "cat restaurant" or a "cathouse," the latter meaning a house of ill-fame and the former is a restaurant where loose women cat. In wider application of the term, "cat" is applied generally to women, though it restricted among the more aesthetic criminals to loose women. A blow of the fist or club is a "slug." The act of stealing is called "swiping." A police officer as everybody knows is a "cop," and, as is equally well known, captured plunder is called "swag."

Handcuffs of course called "bracelets," a thief is a "crook," and the jail is the "jug." A pickpocket is a "dip," and a purse a "poke." Therefore, if a man steals a purse from a pocket, he is said to "dip a poke."

The girls of Guy Town had their own ways of getting whatever they could get, whenever they wanted. Booze was usually involved. The *Statesman* warned in August 1880, "It's not always safe to go down into the First Ward with a large sum of money."

Country girls may have been easy prey for white slavers, but country guys were easy prey for the girls of Guy Town. A nice young countryman, with plenty of money, came to Austin one day in July 1880 with an earnest longing to take in the town and see the sights. He procured a carriage and set out to learn something of the ways that are dark. He rode around all afternoon, taking in at regular intervals schooners of beer until he was boozy and serenely indifferent as to who or where he was. In this condition, he was driven to Fannie Kelley's; taking into the carriage Frankie Howard, they started out on a moonlight ride. They were out until three o'clock in the morning, when they returned to Fannie Kelley's, entered the house and ordered wine for two.

The fascinating Frankie requested the nice young man to foot the bill. Instantly his hand was down into his pants pocket, and instantly it was out again and into another. From there, it was into all the pockets he had about him, while a ghastly look of goneness spread itself over his countenance. He missed a purse containing $480 and at once accused Frankie of having picked his pocket while in the carriage. She vehemently proclaimed her innocence, and she, the nice young man and Fannie Kelley carefully searched the room, but no purse could be found. The young man then declared his unalterable intention of searching Frankie, who positively refused to undergo the ordeal, whereupon the nice young man sent for an officer, but before he arrived, Frankie concluded to let Fannie Kelley search her. It was done, but no money purse was found. Strange to say, however, someone in the room peering around did discover it under the bed, where, just a few minutes before, the combined eyes of Fannie Kelley, Frankie, the nice young man and the carriage driver had failed to see it. It was examined, and the $480 was safe, the wine was paid for and Frankie—who it was believed had the purse about her person and during the search had contrived to get rid of it and kicked it under the bed—was arrested by the policeman who had arrived. She was conducted to the lockup, but the next morning, the nice young man refused to put in an appearance and make a complaint, and Frankie was released from custody.

Another unnamed fellow was in from the rural "deestricks" one day in late September 1888. He browsed around the town, finally ending up at Mollie Seymour's ranch on Fourth Street. Here he fell into the hands of Pearl Clifford, a "painted sepulchre" of the dive, and here he was coolly robbed of a twenty-dollar gold piece and ten dollars in currency. He was asleep during the process, but fortunately for him, he woke up just in the nick of time and saw Pearl relieving him of the gold piece, with which she fled from the room. He demanded it, but she calmly swore that she didn't have it. Of course she so swore. They always did.

He persisted and finally notified Officers Gassoway and Musgrove, and they at once started on a voyage of discovery through the ranch. They discovered nothing, but determining not to be outwitted, they chucked the Pearl of Fourth Street into the cooler.

They went back and renewed their search, and strange to say, between the mattresses of a bed in Pearl's room, they found the twenty-dollar gold piece. It was strange because just prior to marching Pearl to the station, they had examined her room, carefully turned up the mattresses and found nothing. Now the coin was found exactly where no coin was when the first search was made. How did it get there? Pearl was in the lockup, and she didn't place it there. The officers returned the money to the rural rooster, who greatly rejoiced. The next morning, as was so often the case, the "sucker" declined to press charges, preferring anonymity to public humiliation. As for Pearl? As you will read elsewhere, she paid the ultimate price for her indiscretion a little more than two months later.

There was even that "Old Black Magic." In August 1885, Guy Town was all agog over the actions of Antonino Santillo, an Italian only recently arrived in this country. He had been living with a Mexican woman, "Wahna," and Guy Town's Italians claimed that she possessed the power of the witches and that she had conjured Santillo. The Italian immigration agent here had recently received a letter from the mayor of the town where Santillo's family resided, stating that he must remit to his family money for their support. Santillo said that he would like to do so, but Wahna, who now controlled his destiny, said that he must think of his family as belonging with the dead; she had him so completely under her control that he could not help himself. All the Mexicans and Italians in Austin were afraid to go around where this woman was, firmly convinced that she had the power to do them harm, and it would take a persuasive six-shooter to make any of them go to her house.

One reason why there was so much no-good going on was that there were never enough police officers to police Guy Town. In January 1882, only one policeman was compelled to do duty there, and he spent most of his time keeping the peace at Charley Cunio's.

Not that there was much one officer could do; on the night of July 16, 1884, Officer Howe, in passing by Alf Morris's lunch stand, better known as the "Hard Man's Hole" and a rendezvous for the hardest characters in Austin, found several women of color sitting on the sidewalk. He told them to buy whatever they wanted and move on, as they were violating the law in remaining there. Pete Tigue, a burly black man, confronted Officer Howe, asking him what business it was of his whether they left or not.

Officer Howe replied that it was his business, as an officer of the law, to see the law enforced, and as this was contrary to the law, his order must be obeyed. Tigue informed the officer that he could not make the women leave and that he was running that part of town himself. Seeing himself well backed by forty or fifty of his peers, he proceeded to defy the officer, cursing him and the entire police force generally. Officer Howe saw that he was at too great a disadvantage to do anything and withdrew for assistance. Reinforced by Marshal Lee and Officer Lausen, he returned, and they took Tigue in charge and deposited him in the cooler. There was no disguising the fact that the city had a small nighttime police force.

Just a few months earlier, the *Statesman* had complained, "The night police force is ridiculously small. Four men to guard the property of 16,000 people! One to every 4,000, and one to every 8,000 after midnight!" Frequently there was only one man to guard the peace of the entire city. This deplorable fact had given Austin a reputation for lawlessness not only in Texas but also throughout the nation. Hard Man's Hole was just a few doors north of the Gem Saloon, where young James Simms was shot and died in 1880.

The startling clang of the fire bell woke many citizens at three o'clock in morning on February 20, 1885. The *Statesman* reported, "The whole first ward was illuminated with a vivid, brilliant glow and the blaze cast a bright glare over the squalid tenements inhabited by shameless women and depraved men of the lowest stamp. The flames had enveloped in their charitable embrace that odoriferous and wayward haunt known as the Gem Saloon. The destroyed house had been the scene of some of the most outrageous orgies and reckless revels that ever made night hideous. No tears were shed for its loss."

CHAPTER 10
ROUGH HOUSE ROYALTY

Fights in Guy Town were as regular as rain forest downpours—scarcely a night without one. There were heavy hitters among Austin's "frail ones," like Emma Tweedle, but they all paled in the face of Lottie Stotts, Austin's "Queen of the Toughs." Lottie was by common acclaim the toughest woman in town and tougher than most men. Lottie's rages began in 1880 and seem to have been spurred by the conviction and imprisonment of her second husband for miscegenation in 1879. She was arrested at least three dozen times in twelve years, mostly for intoxication and assault but also for disturbing the peace, theft, abusive language and threatening arson—never for vagrancy (a charge often leveled at prostitutes), though she was referred to as a prostitute in the arrest records several times.

On March 18, 1879, Emile Francois, an immigrant French mattress maker, and Lottie Stotts, described as a "mulatto woman," were joined in the union of holy matrimony. The two had been witnesses in a case on trial in Justice Fritz Tegener's court, in the course of which it became known that Francois and Lottie were living in adultery. Threatened with prosecution, Francois married Lottie and, by so doing, escaped the frying pan only to land in the state penitentiary. He was charged with violating the Texas statute of 1858 that banned interracial marriage, a law that was in conflict with the Fourteenth Amendment and thus regarded by many legal authorities outside Texas as null and void. Francois claimed to be part black, but medical experts who examined him declared this to be untrue. Lottie was the mother of two half-grown girls (Ida and Flora) at the time.

In July 1879 in district court, Emile Francois was convicted of marrying a "negress" and given five years' hard labor in the Huntsville State Penitentiary. As the *Daily Statesman* described, "The devoted wife of Francois was present during the trial, and when the jury pronounced the verdict, she fell upon his shoulder, and wept forth streams of love, and made more noise than a colored camp meeting. Francois will appeal, if for nothing else than to encourage his darling to love him still. In the colored marriage code, confinement in the penitentiary is accepted as a decree of divorce, and Francois couldn't afford to lose her. He couldn't get another like her, and she could not find another Francois."

Lottie's first appearance in print came on January 11, 1880, when she was convicted of disturbing the peace and was fined five dollars and costs. By August 1881, her fame was such that the *Statesman* commented that "international opera diva Emma Abbott is inventing a new kiss, and Lottie a new kick."

Lottie caused more trouble to the policemen and constables in Austin than any two individuals who ever lived in this city. She probably spent at least two-thirds of her life in Austin in the city prison. To wit: "Lottie Stotts, whose reputation for general cussedness is as black as her dark complected skin, is in jail again," the *Statesman* reported on June 1, 1882. "She got on a drunk yesterday and kicked up a muss, for which the police took her in." Lottie was fined twenty dollars, but owing to her inability to pay, she was committed to jail.

She served her two weeks and was arrested again on June 16. After being carried to the jail, she set up such a howl as to force the officials to chain her down. She was fined twenty-five dollars. While in jail serving out that fine, Lottie lodged a complaint against Henrietta Hardeman and Emma Whipple, charging them with kidnapping one of her daughters. After nearly two months in jail, Lottie was hired out to a local cotton planter.

By April 1883, Lottie was free again, but not for long; she was arrested on April 18 for drunkenness. One night in September 1883, Lottie took a bottle and tried to break a hole in a poor crippled boy's head. After several more enforced vacations, Lottie was again passing the time away in city jail when, on November 13, 1883, a handyman left the back door unbolted, and four male prisoners took "French leave."

Lottie, for reasons known only to herself, declined to join them. In August 1884, Texas governor John Ireland granted Francois a pardon, but since the pardon did not restore his citizenship rights, Francois refused it and filed suit against Governor Ireland, charging him with conspiring to defraud him

"The Huntsville State Penitentiary." *Author's collection.*

out of his rights of citizenship. A federal marshal was sent to arrest Ireland, producing no result. The affair drew national headlines.

As all of this unfolded, Lottie was in jail, where she said that she hoped that Francois would not be liberated; she was also indignant that he should have been the occasion of any annoyance to the governor. While her wish in regard to Francois was echoed in the hearts of the authorities in this city, they added to it by hoping that Lottie would soon join Francois as a companion in prison, if not as the companion of his bosom. They never did reconcile.

Several chapters of this book could be spent chronicling the exploits of Lottie Stotts, but this November 1884 story from the *Statesman* sums it all up best:

> *Perhaps it was a benign fate that sent Emile Francois to Huntsville, instead of compelling him to pass his days with that female terror, the redoubtable Lottie Stotts. Of all the hard characters in Austin she will easily take the blue ribbon for innate deviltry and general cussedness. When under the influence of liquor, which is her usual state, she is as reckless of life as a lioness thirsty for gore, and there is nothing that she will not dare. She seems scarcely human in her awful rage, and no efforts of the policemen can subdue her. Last night, about 11 o'clock, assisted by her daughter, Flora, and a Mexican woman named Julia, she gave another Mexican female, a chronic offender*

also, named Annie Lyons, a terrible beating. The three women all jumped on the other and pummeled her so severely that the outcries and racket brought Officer John Bracken and special policeman Jim Williams to the scene. The arrest of all three followed, and they were about to be taken to the station, when Lottie Stotts requested Bracken to let her go in her room for a pair of shoes. He agreed, and followed her in. The room was lighted only by the rays of the moon and the officer turned to strike a match. As he did so, Williams, who was at the entrance, saw the woman raise a piece of scantling, then before he could arrest the blow, she dealt Bracken a severe stroke on the head. It knocked him entirely out of the house, and he fell in his comrade's arms. Hardly had the arrested parties been locked up in a cell, when a scream from Julia, followed by the most horrible imprecations and curses ever listened to, announced that this diabolical negress had not yet finished her work, had not yet glutted her satanic thirst for gore. Very quickly unlocking the door Officer Boyce found the woman Julia, bleeding profusely from an ugly looking cut on her forehead. She explained that it was Lottie's work, and that a bottle was the instrument used.

The reporter seldom saw a more revolting sight than the scene presented: The Mexican woman, herself not more elevated in the scale of humanity than her assailant, shedding hideous tears over her suffering; in the other room the doctor busily attending to the hurt policeman; two or three prisoners gazing around, with a half drunken, stupid stare; and inside this cell the fiend that caused the trouble swearing the most horrible oaths against everybody and everything. It is likely, though, that this affair may yet result in ridding the community of a most desperate character, as Officer Bracken will most likely prosecute her for an assault with intent to murder. Maybe Francois' place in Huntsville will yet be occupied by his former wife, "a consummation devoutly to be wished."

Lottie pleaded guilty to aggravated assault on Officer Bracken, and the jury gave her six months in the county jail.

At about 7:30 p.m. the evening of October 6, 1886, Lottie got filled up with fighting whiskey and proceeded to take to the First Ward with a knife. At the corner of Third and Colorado Streets, she stabbed a white man through the hand and then repaired to Tilda Barnhart's house and demolished and threw the furniture into the street—at which she succeeded admirably, until Officer Gibson put in an appearance and arrested her. She cursed the officer in the most vile manner and would have used her knife had not the officer threatened her with his six-shooter.

On their way to the police station, she kept quiet until she was within the hearing of respectable ladies on the street. She would then curse and use the worst low, indecent language that could be imagined. "It is a disgrace to the city to allow such people to remain within its limits," the *Statesman* chided.

Lottie was also Austin's first resident cross-dresser, often going out for a night on the town in men's clothing. Unlike drug use and prostitution, cross-dressing was a crime at the time, but somehow it just didn't seem worth the trouble to get Lottie riled up over wearing a pair of men's trousers and a sack coat.

Lottie had a thoroughbred stable of miscreant offspring: Ida, Flora, Henry and Lloyd. Each got into his or her share of troubles, but of the quartet, Ida was purentee triple crown. Ida Stotts first appears on the Austin scene on June 15, 1882, when she and Albert Doyle were arraigned in court on a charge of adultery. Ida was about fourteen years of age and the boy probably a year younger. Justice Tegener dismissed the case on general principle and because there was no evidence to sustain the charge. About one year earlier, Ida had married a "full-grown negro" but left him and went back to her mother after living with him about a week. The husband tried every means to get her back but failed; he then brought the charge of adultery and sued for a divorce.

One month later, Albert Doyle had her arrested for cursing him. In August, Ida and a young pal, Henrietta Hardeman (who had celebrated her twelfth birthday in jail on a charge of theft), were arrested and fined for indecent exposure, a common charge filed against *nymphs du pave*.

Ida would go on to get arrested at least a dozen more times during the rest of the 1880s for such other offenses as disturbing the peace, assault, vagrancy, drunkenness and prostitution before moving to San Antonio's red-light district, where she died a mysterious death in 1893. The *Statesman's* attitude toward Lottie mellowed somewhat with time, as this note from December 30, 1890, illustrates:

> *Aunt Lottie Stotts is a character in this city and sometimes goes on the warpath. With all her faults, however, she is generous and many are her acts of charity. Her house was robbed a few nights ago of nearly $50 worth of clothing. The robbery was traced to a Mexican named Adame and he was arrested and a part of the clothing was recovered. Adame is in jail.*

Lottie began to mellow perhaps because she was getting tired of the wild life. As the Gay Nineties set in, her appearances in court became less frequent and for more benign offenses, such as drunkenness and theft.

On August 7, 1892, Lottie was convicted of disturbing the peace and, unable to pay the ten-dollar fine, was again confined to Austin's bastille on the hill. Enough was enough, evidently, and Lottie decided to join the angels on the afternoon of August 18, using a large quantity of morphine that she had concealed on her person. Dr. Graves managed to pull Lottie around, but as soon as she got out of jail, she got outrageously drunk and was arrested, convicted and thrown again into the clink. Lottie moved, soon after, to San Antonio to join daughter Ida, where she finally succeeded in dying of a morphine overdose on April 2, 1896.

If Lottie Stotts was the "Queen of Toughs" in Guy Town, Charley Cunio (or Cuneo or Cuny or Cuney or Cooney, as he was variously called) was the magnate of that part of Guy Town known as Mexico, or Cooneyville. He was arrested at least as many times as Lottie, but his wiliness kept him out of jail.

This Italian immigrant arrived in Austin sometime after the Civil War and began to acquire property in the west part of the First Ward, at Nueces and Third Streets near the present-day hike-and-bike trail bridge over Shoal Creek. The neighborhood that grew up around it was overwhelmingly Mexican, although customers of all colors attended Charley's bar and dance hall—hence the area being known as "Mexico."

Charley first made headlines in August 1870, when Preciliana Castro filed a complaint against him for having used profane and offensive language to her. It was the first of many court appearances to come over the next twenty or so years, for charges ranging from disturbing the peace to simple assault (of both men and women), assault with intent to murder, carrying a pistol, gambling, abusive language, robbery, building a house without a permit, cursing a police officer and cutting a police officer.

His compound quickly became infamous for the fandangos held there. They got so rowdy that in March 1874, several citizens of the First Ward petitioned the city council to suppress them. After considerable debate, "the city marshal was authorized and instructed to suppress and close" all houses where lewd men and women or persons who have no visible means of support meet for the purpose of "fandangoing" and the like.

The 1875 census listed him as fifty years old, single, illiterate and a "speculator" by trade. Charley may have been illiterate, but he was well acquainted with the finer points of the law. To wit: There was quite a lively scrimmage on May 17, 1876, in Judge Neill's court between the district attorney and Charley, the "drill major and orderly sergeant" of Mexico. Charley had a friend on trial and was having pretty nearly as much to say

Cooneyville (center, north of the railroad tracks). *From* Austin, State Capital of Texas, *drawn by August Koch, 1887. Author's collection.*

A Mexican kitchen. *Author's collection.*

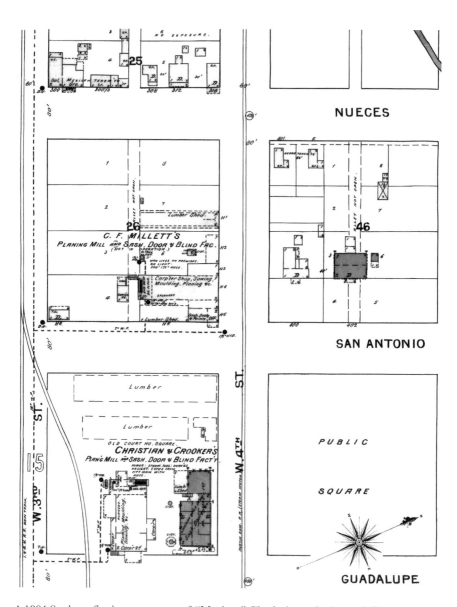

A 1894 Sanborn fire insurance map of "Mexican" Charley's rancho (upper left).

in the case as the district attorney. Charley finally got inside the railing among the lawyers and witnesses and there again offered a little advice calculated to disturb the court and break the district attorney's thread of argument. Apparently anxious that Charley should also be made familiar with law, the district attorney picked up a copy of Blackstone and sent it whizzing at Charley's head, where it stopped on the southwest corner of Charley's cranium, causing a lump about the size of a "Mexican biscuit." Charley then "lit out," and the district attorney was fined ten dollars for contempt of court, order was restored and the trial continued. Presently Charley returned, looking as savage as a Mexican lion though making no warlike demonstrations. However, he commenced wending his way closer and closer to the party who had tried to pound a little law into him, and finally Officer George walked up and took hold of Charley—under his coat, he found about a foot and a half of pistol. Charley pleaded guilty to carrying concealed weapons, and he was fined, and after the court adjourned, he made a charge against the district attorney for assault and battery.

A *Statesman* reporter made the mistake of calling Charley a "Mexican" when reporting on one of his many scrapes in March 1887:

> *Charles Cunio is a Mexican who lives in the first ward, and who, all in all, bears a reputation none too savory. Constable Thorp, a few days ago, had a warrant against him, charging him with assault and battery. Going to his place to execute it, Cunio went upstairs, barred his door and began cursing and abusing the officer, threatening to kill him if he entered the premises. The officer proposed to enter, when the Mexican agreed to surrender and present himself at court the next morning. As he is a property owner, his recognizance was taken. The next day, however, he went off to Lockhart, and has since managed to keep out of Thorp's way, until yesterday. To evade being yanked without ceremony, he went up to Justice Calhoun and entered into bonds for his appearance next Monday to answer for his misdemeanors.*

A few days later, the *Statesman* apologized, sort of, for its inaccuracy: "Charles Cunio, of whose arrest mention was made a day or so ago, indignantly denies that he is a Mexican, and wishes it to be distinctly understood that he is an Italian. All right, a cheerful apology is hereby extended—to the Mexicans."

Charley's saloon was always a lively place, even when there were no fandangos: fistfights, knifings and shootings were weekly and sometimes daily affairs. Amazingly, only one police officer was detailed for the First

Ward, and all his energies were usually required to keep the peace at Charley Cunio's store.

Charley had achieved considerable local fame for his ability to wiggle out of legal troubles. On May 28, 1882, the *Statesman* reported that "[a] member of the Austin bar says that Charley, though he can neither read nor write, is a better lawyer than any the state can procure to prosecute him."

Lottie Stotts was a regular at Charley's saloon. In a row there on the evening of January 28, 1882, Alex Arregon cut Lottie. The wound was not very serious, and Arregon was arrested and jailed. Lottie and Charley also engaged in wordy warfare there on June 29, 1883, that cost each of them five dollars.

Lottie Stotts was the toughest gal in Guy Town, but Lola Smith was a legitimate contender for the crown. She fought like a man and drank whiskey until she could see stars in a lamppost. Not many men got the best of Charley Cunio, but on March 15, 1884, Lola called on Charley and proposed to thrash him in half a minute, and she did it. Charley had her arrested for whipping him, and she had him arrested for letting himself get whipped.

Some of the girls were as good with a knife as the baddest boys. Between twelve o'clock and one o'clock on July 23, 1887, Josie Brown, a white woman, was standing in the doorway of Cunio's corral when a Mexican woman named Julia Braun dashed up to her and, without warning, made a savage lunge at her with a knife. The blade struck her wrist, glanced and inflicted two ugly gashes on her abdomen. The blade then skewed downward, missed the groin and laid bare the thigh in a wound about six inches long. Brown screamed and fell, and her assailant escaped into the darkness. Braun was recognized and captured soon after.

By the summer of 1894, Charley was nearing seventy years of age and was but a shell of the scrapper he had been. At nearly dusk on the evening of August 23, J.C. Campbell was arrested for creating a disturbance. Campbell had taken it into his head to possess Charley's store, and with that object in view, he drove Cunio and his daughter out, cursing them rather vigorously. Charley sent for the police. Upon their arrival, Campbell was seen standing across the street.

Officer Corwin approached him and informed him that he must accompany him to the station, as Charley had charged him with disorderly conduct. After a short talk, Campbell, who was a large, muscular man, shook loose from Officer Corwin, who had hold of his arm, and picked up two rocks, looking to do Charley up. Officer Corwin grabbed him by the collar almost immediately and prevented his doing Cunio any harm. Campbell turned so viciously on Corwin, however, that Corwin was compelled to use his pistol as a club and knock Campbell down. Campbell was up almost as soon as he hit the ground, and then he and Corwin had a wrestling match themselves. Officer Scott, who was also there, took a hand in the proceedings, and after a little scrapping, the two officers succeeded in overpowering Campbell and taking him to the station.

After this incident, Charley fades from the scene. No further mention of him appears in local newspapers, and there is no record of his death or burial in city records.

Guy Town began to fade from the scene about this time, too, at least by that name in the newspapers. The houses of prostitution enjoyed a steady business until 1913, but as *The Rolling Stone* pointed out on April 13, 1894, the gambling and violence had moved from Guy Town to East Sixth Street, where it would remain until the Sixth Street renaissance of the 1970s and 1980s: "It behooves the bloody First Ward to stir its stumps if it wishes to keep the belt for being a tough locality. East Pecan and the vicinity, once the center of business, where the mild-eyed granger traded eggs and butter for the delusive calico, and drank his red lemonade in peace, has now risen up and declared itself bold, bad and hard to curry. Loafing, gambling, fighting and drinking have invaded this Arcadian spot. Let us pass some more laws against this kind of thing and then let it go on as usual."

CHAPTER 11
CHERCHEZ LA FEMME, CHERCHEZ L'HOMME

C herchez la femme" is a French phrase that means "look for the woman" and comes from the 1854 novel *The Mohicans of Paris*, by Alexandre Dumas. Dumas used an expanded version ("*Il y a une femme dans toutes les affaires; aussitôt qu'on me fait un rapport, je dis: 'Cherchez la femme!'*") in his 1864 theatrical adaptation of the book, which, translated into English, means, "There is a woman in every case; as soon as they bring me a report, I say, 'Look for the woman!'"

The phrase was adopted into everyday English use and crossed the Atlantic in the early 1900s. It was well known enough by 1909 that O. Henry (William Sydney Porter) used it as the title of a story that includes this line: "Ah! yes, I know most time when those men lose money you say 'Cherchez la femme'—there is somewhere the woman."

Why do fools fall in love? Why did Guy Town hookers and johns fall in love? And often in the triangular fashion? In Guy Town, the "green-eyed monster" of jealousy worked both ways: look for the woman; look for the man.

On the evening of November 8, 1871, Jack Hunter, a state policeman notorious for his lawless acts (such as forgery), got a buggy and started to visit the mayor's residence on business in the company of the fair Minnie Rives. The day being bright and lovely, no dream was entertained but that of love and happiness. But "the course of true love never runs smooth," and Jack and Minnie soon discovered this to their sorrow. Jack was a very lovable gentleman, for as he neared the worthy mayor's residence, he was met by the mortified Flora Temple, who, not able to endure the pangs of jealousy

Alexandre Dumas. *In the public domain.*

and the mortification of seeing the adorable Jack in the company of a rival, fell on Jack with her delicate hands and in her blind fury gave poor Jack a most merciless whipping. He was left badly bruised, with numerous fingers broken, and he and his heartbroken Flora were forced to explain, as well as they could, such indiscretion before the public.

About half-past one o'clock in the morning of September 13, 1883, the First Ward was the scene of another tragedy, somewhere in between the Gem Saloon and the "Hard Man's Hole." Bull Creek Annie Hamilton was the moving cause. Bob Lotterdale, a roving blade from Dripping Springs, was deeply smitten by the charms of gentle Annie, and he had come to the capital city that night to pay court to her. But when he called on "my lady," she was basking in the sunlight of George Sharp's smiling countenance. Lotterdale did not like that, taking deep offense that Sharp had been going to see "his Anna," and he hinted that two fellows could not court one girl at the same time—not if he was one of them. He went away, but returned later and met George and Anna on the street. He ran up against Sharp in an insulting way,

Left: William S. Porter. *In the public domain.*

Below: Bull Creek. *Author's collection.*

126

and Sharp resented it. This appears to be just what Lotterdale wanted, and the two men began to use the most profane and indecent language toward the other. When this reached a certain point, Lotterdale drew his pistol and put the muzzle right over Sharp's heart and fired. The ball struck a rib and followed it around, inflicting only a flesh wound. Lotterdale fired two other shots at Sharp and then fled. The police heard the firing and went promptly to the scene, but Lotterdale had made his escape before they arrived.

On the evening of November 2, 1881, between eight o'clock and nine o'clock, George Carpenter, a black man and barber by trade, found John Stokes, another black man, in his darkened house, intent on burglary or illicit intercourse with the wife. Stokes rushed past Carpenter and out at the front door. Carpenter followed him, and four shots were exchanged, Stokes being wounded in both legs, although not dangerously. Carpenter was arrested, and his trial soon commenced. But after reviewing the facts, the prosecuting and county attorneys moved for a dismissal of the case.

Jacob Basil, said to be a native of Arabia or Turkey, came to Austin from Houston sometime in mid-March 1892. A wholesale dealer in the garish gewgaws that "Arabian" peddlers sold on the streets, Basil was here to see about his bills and other things, and he soon fell head over heels in love with the dark-eyed, prepossessing wife of Amenta Henez. To Jacob's infinite joy, his love was returned, and the two became very intimate and were often in each other's company, when they should have been as far apart as the police, stretched thin as they were on the streets.

Amenta Henez waxed jealous, and he swooped down on Basil "Bedouin fashion" and had him arrested and arraigned on a charge of stealing his wife's affections. The earlier chapter "Mixing the Colors" described how men and women of differing races and ethnicities intermingled freely during Guy Town's heyday, and the following two incidents illustrate how the "green-eyed monster" of jealousy ignored color lines.

Fannie Powell, a black dove, was suddenly stricken with a severe attack of jealousy on the evening of May 6, 1880, and undertook the pleasing task of demolishing the object of her feelings, Mamie Campbell, a white dove (who in the course of her career roomed with Sallie Daggett and Blanche Dumont). Fannie punched Mamie's head and, to make things still livelier, furiously assailed a Mr. H. Glass, the center of the fête a trois, who returned the favor in a manner contrary to law. He also tore around and smashed the door lock, battered the door and otherwise badly used up the whole house, and altogether they succeeded admirably in kicking up one of the most cheerful musses that Mexico had seen in quite some time.

A remarkable case of mistaken identity (or absent-mindedness, or whatever one might call it) occurred one Sunday night in December 1882. A gentleman of color, whose wife was the cook of a certain businessman, went home to his virtuous family somewhat late in the night, and as he went to his bed, he was startled to find that there was no room for him. His wife was there peacefully dreaming, and so was someone else. The husband began to think that he himself was dreaming too. There was a man in the bed, but it wasn't himself or his double, for the intruding party was a white man. The gentleman had always believed that he was the proper and only authorized person to rest in the bosom of his family, and consequently, he prepared for a raid. But just at that moment, the other party awoke and discovered his mistake, realizing that he was one too many. There could be no more sweet dreams in that house, for there was blood in the husband's eye. The chances were good that in a very few moments, the roof would take a trip to the stars. The white man didn't argue the case but instead broke for the window and liberty, out into the cool night air. But alas for him! He had left his clothes with the contestant, and it was not at all the kind of night for roaming around with nothing but underwear on. The husband gathered up the other's articles of attire— boots, stockings, trousers, vest, coat, hat and gloves—and carried them to the police station, where they were put on exhibition.

Nearly a week later, the outfit still remained there, unclaimed and causing considerable vexation. There was a pungency that had an unpleasant effect on sensitive nostrils when one got close to the peg where they hung. "Charity should pervade everything," the *Statesman* advised, "and it is out of charity to the unhappy city officers that we ask the owner of those clothes to carry them away and out of sight and hearing," and also that he not inter the wardrobe inside the Austin corporate limits or sink them in the Colorado River above the city's water pumps.

"The husband of the cook-lady who was somewhat connected with this suit of clothes, has expressed himself as desirous of procuring a divorce, which, if carried out, will leave the ebony-colored damsel somewhat forsaken and alone in the world. Now it seems that she might go to the station house and get the clothes referred to, thus securing herself something with which to console herself in her widowhood. To her they might prove not only ornamental but useful; and they would remind her of happy hours in the past that can never return," the *Statesman* concluded.

And then there was Maud. Maud James didn't have much luck when it came to men. A serious cutting affray occurred at about 3:30 p.m. on June

5, 1890, between Hattie Starr and Maud. Both women were in love with the same man. Soon after the disturbance, Maud was arrested and taken before Justice Calhoun. An examination was waived, and she was released on bond of $500, Mr. T.N. Miller being her bondsman. She claimed that when she first met Hattie Starr in the office of her lover, she was received with a storm of oaths and curses. She at once left the room but was followed home by Hattie, who again commenced to quarrel and struck her over the head with a parasol, breaking it by the blow. Maud cuttingly returned the favor, compelled to do it in self-defense.

Maud first cut Hattie in the eye, and then a severe thrust sent the keen blade of Maud's dagger downward into the left chest. Another slash went in the left side, and had it not been for Hattie's corset, it might have proved fatal. After the cutting, Hattie was put in a hack and was driven to Dr. Church's office, where her wounds were dressed. There she told her story to a reporter:

> *I have been living with a man here in town about four or five years and have been recognized as his wife. A short time ago I left the city on a brief visit and on returning found that he had gone to live with Maud James and would not come near me. This morning I went to see him and while I was talking I saw Maud James coming up the stairs. I told her not to come into the room and after a few words she left the house. In a short time I started for Maud's house to see her and explain matters. No sooner had I entered the yard gate than she saw me and ran toward me and at once began to cut me without saying a word. We were then separated by the man who caused the trouble.*

It was election week in November 1888, and George Sharp got tanked up on the afternoon of November 6 and conceived a brilliant plan to relieve the monotony of election times. He proceeded to Mollie Seymour's house, where he beat Maud with a bed slat over the head, and not finding that satisfactory, he slashed her in the side with a small knife. He would have done so with a large one but didn't happen to have one about him. After he had succeeded in pounding up Maud pretty well, Officer DeFraisses, with the aid of several police officers, succeeded in landing Sharp in the cooler after much effort. Maud was very painfully but not seriously injured.

Maud may have won her battle with Hattie Starr, but in the end, she lost the war, as the *Statesman* headlines blared on October 13, 1891:

The Same End.
A Life of Shame Leads Ever to the Grave.

It's a path which always leads to the same end, no matter how it may wander, no matter how it may hide its tortuous way among the false flowers which often deck a life of shame. Maud James was once an honest and respected maiden. It is but a few short years since she was the light of a happy home. But she fell. Today the grave closes above her silent form. It was about 4 o'clock yesterday afternoon a little boy returning from school happened to glance into the dilapidated cottage back of Cuneo's store on Colorado and Third streets, opposite the depot. The sight he beheld filled him with horror. A woman lay dying there.

The little fellow hastened for assistance and then it was found that Maud James was the unfortunate, the victim of an overdose of morphine. Doctors did everything that human power could do to save the waning life, but all was in vain. Death claimed his own within an hour.

The remnants of the morphine were there, but there was nothing—no letter, no word or token—to tell whether it was a case of suicide, or anyone to detail the circumstances if it was an accident.

Maud James had been one of Mollie Seymour's inmates and was but twenty-two years old at the time of her demise.

CHAPTER 12
ONE LUMP OR THREE?

Mexico sans mayhem would have been like the Sahara without sand. In its prime, scarcely a night passed in Guy Town without some kind of physical violence. Man against man, man versus woman, *nymph contra nymph*.

By the end of June 1876, the *Statesman* observed:

> *Hardly a Saturday night rolls around but there is a serious and bloody altercation down in "Mexico," and people have come to look for a murder down in the vicinity every Saturday night. The very worst and most reckless people congregate in that part of the city, and especially on Saturday night, when disgraceful and noisy dance establishments are thrown open to add to the other attractions pleasing to lovers of vice and boisterous excitement. On Saturday night a man named J.J. Barton, from New Orleans, and who had been in this city several weeks, stepped into a saloon opposite Charley Cooney's and asked for a gun, but it being denied him he stepped out and leaned against a post, and was talking to someone. In a minute more a report was heard and a flash seen half a block distant, and Barton dropped dead where he was standing, a ball having passed through his head. Barton had quarreled with a man named Charles Wilson, who, it is said, had threatened his life, and Wilson has been arrested to answer for the crime of Barton's murder.*

Wilson was ultimately found innocent.

Most altercations in Guy Town were spontaneous, but some had been a long time coming. They were all fueled by generous doses of bad whiskey,

A Guy Town–era saloon. *Courtesy of Austin History Center.*

Austin City Hospital. *Author's collection.*

as the *Statesman* explained, tongue in cheek, in June 1882: "Lower Avenue whiskey is pugnacious. Upper Avenue whiskey is loquacious and sentimental. East Pecan liquor, maudlin lachrymose—one drink a propensity to swear and wipe somebody, two drinks madness, four drinks death and damnation. First ward decoctions, fed profusely to the troops, inspire them with a disposition to fight nobly and break into the penitentiary generally."

Bird Penn, a black man with a reputation notorious even by Guy Town standards, had an altercation on the evening of October 23, 1882, with Z.T. Perino, who kept a First Ward lunch counter. After some very strong language, Perino cracked Penn's head with a pepper-sauce bottle. As Penn stepped back to get a chance to draw his pistol, more bottles began to fly. Penn got three ugly cuts near the left eye and managed to waste four bullets in missing his man. He was fined forty dollars and costs for packing a pistol, while Perino got off with a fine of ten dollars.

On July 3, 1890, at about six o'clock in the afternoon, a crowd gathered in front of Hugh Hancock's on Colorado Street, near the International depot, was listening to a band. The band was playing its best, and people in the crowd were keeping time with their feet when the report of a six-shooter was heard, quickly followed by another. A black man rushed from the crowd, running up Colorado Street in the direction of California Frank's, followed by a black teenage boy who continued to pop away with his six-shooter at the man ahead of him.

About in front of California Frank's, the man in the lead, bleeding freely, stopped until his assailant, who was still firing, came up. The two grappled and struggled desperately for possession of the six-shooter for some moments until the wounded man succeeded in wrenching the pistol from the other's hands. At that moment, Officer Pace pounced down on them and promptly arrested the younger man, while the other, desperately wounded, struggled into a wagon and asked to be conveyed to the city hospital, saying, "I am badly shot."

The young man arrested gave his name as Emanuel McGar and stated that the man he shot, John Oliver, had stabbed and killed his father seven years earlier near Hempstead, Texas. Oliver was arrested and tried but got off because McGar was the attacking party and he had fired one or two shots before Oliver used his knife.

Emanuel, then about twelve years old, swore vengeance, and upon meeting Oliver for the first time since his father's death, he proceeded to fill him with lead without warning. He fired five shots, three taking effect, one passing through the liver and the others grazing the neck.

Who said that there is no honor among bad guys? When the police came around Guy Town, no one talked, alive or dead.

A crowd of men was having a general drunken frolic one afternoon in February 1884 in Charley Cunio's saloon when an Italian and a man named Gonzales got into some difficulty. Gonzales was seriously cut about the back and abdomen, deep enough to allow the intestines to drop out. The police officers were soon on the scene of action, and the disturbance was quelled. The Italian was arrested and jailed. "There is one thing strange about the citizens in that locality of the city," the *Statesman* noted in its report on the affair. "When any difficulty occurs there is no person that knows anything about it. Even the parties present are particularly reticent in the matter, and offenders of the law would go unpunished were it not for the men who represent the police powers of the city."

The only celebrity tussle in Guy Town involved City Marshal Ben Thompson and Johnny Ringo, of Tombstone, Arizona fame. Bat Masterson said of Thompson, "It is very doubtful if, in his time, there was another man living who equaled him with the pistol in a life and death struggle. The very name of Ben Thompson was enough to cause the general run of 'man killers,' even those who had never seen him, to seek safety in instant flight."

Ringo was passing his time down in a house in the jungles of Guy Town early Sunday morning, May 1, 1881. Along about four o'clock, he missed his purse, and stepping out in the hall, where some three or four of Austin's nice young men were seated, he came down on them with his pistol and commanded them to "up hands." Then he searched them. Not finding his purse, he retired to his room, while they quietly slid out and reported the facts to the police. Marshal Thompson went down to the house and, when refused admission to the room, cheerfully kicked open the door. To Ringo's infinite disgust, Thompson scooped him in. He was disarmed, marched to the station and the next day fined five dollars and costs for disturbing the peace, as well as twenty-five dollars and costs for carrying a pistol. Ringo settled with the city and left a wiser if not sadder man.

The song "You Only Hurt the One You Love" dates only to World War II, but the sentiment goes way, way back. One March morning in 1880, a Mr. C. Down was in court, charged with assaulting and striking Lula Shaw. "It is strange," the *Statesman* pondered, "that men who voluntarily seek the company of such women deem it their bounden duty to beat and mistreat them. Heaven knows they have a hard life of it at best. Banished from society and thrown out upon the great world as outcasts, to whom no helping hand is ever extended, they go down to an untimely grave,

Ben Thompson. *From* Life and Adventures of Ben Thompson the Famous Texan, *W.M. Walton, 1884.*

overwhelmed with great griefs and sorrow and heartaches that the world is a stranger to."

Why should beating up a prostitute be so surprising when domestic violence among honorably married couples was an accepted fact of life, as illustrated in the O. Henry short story, "A Harlem Tragedy." O. Henry was a connoisseur of the seamy side of life, going back to the days in Austin when he was just Will Porter, visiting Mesdames Sallie Daggett and Georgia Fraser and roaming the back alleys of Guy Town and the rest of Austin, looking, listening and taking stock of life. As Porter wrote, Mrs. Fink dropped into Mrs. Cassidy's flat one flight below:

"I wouldn't have a man," declared Mrs. Cassidy, "that didn't beat me up at least once a week. Shows he thinks something of you. Say! but that last dose Jack gave me wasn't no homeopathic one. I can see stars yet. But he'll be the sweetest man in town for the rest of the week to make up for it. This eye is good for theater tickets and a silk shirt waist at the very least."

"Don't it hurt when he soaks you?" asked Mrs. Fink, curiously.

"Hurt!"—Mrs. Cassidy gave a soprano scream of delight. "Well, say—did you ever have a brick house fall on you?—well, that's just the way it feels. Jack's got a left that spells two matinees and a new pair of Oxfords—and his right!—well, it takes a trip to Coney and six pairs of openwork, silk lisle threads to make that good."

"But what does he beat you for?" inquired Mrs. Fink, with wide-open eyes.

"Silly!" said Mrs. Cassidy, indulgently. "Why, because he's full. It's generally on Saturday nights."

"But what cause do you give him?"

"Why, didn't I marry him? Jack comes in tanked up; and I'm here, ain't I? Who else has he got a right to beat? I'd just like to catch him once beating anybody else! Sometimes it's because supper ain't ready; and sometimes it's because it is. Jack ain't particular about causes. He just lushes till he remembers he's married, and then he makes for home and does me up. Saturday nights I just move the furniture with sharp corners out of the way, so I won't cut my head when he gets his work in. Sometimes I take the count in the first round; but when I feel like having a good time during the week or want some new rags I come up again for more punishment. That's what I done last night. Jack knows I've been wanting a black silk waist for a month, and I didn't think just one black eye would bring it. Tell you what, Mag, I'll bet you the ice cream he brings it to-night."

Jack Cassidy's Guy Town counterparts were seldom so generous afterward with the objects of their affliction. John Nairy met up with Eva Clifton one Wednesday in August 1880. Not overcome with Eva's good looks and dashing appearance, and gathering up a stick, he proceeded to demolish her after the usual style. He was so elated that he concluded to demolish Sallie Daggett and proceeded to kick and break in the door to her room, but before he succeeded, an officer nabbed him, and the next morning, he was fined fifteen dollars and costs, in default of which he was committed.

Those sworn to "serve and protect" did not always do so either. In 1885, the city council had to pass an ordinance prohibiting officers from having fun in the places they were supposed to police. Awful cries of "help"

Here we have Kate and John.
Will Kate fight John or rail
at him?

Oh, no! for Kate loves John.
He bought her a nice ring.

From The Rolling Stone

"My Black-Eyed Girl." *From* The Rolling Stone, *O. Henry, Doubleday, Page and Company, 1918.*

and "murder" aroused the sleeping populace of West Pecan Street on the night of June 19, 1883, and the next morning, Rosa Wilson, an inmate of Sallie Daggett's bagnio, filed a charge of attempted outrage against Police Officer Brown.

Rosa claimed that Brown had taken her on a moonlit buggy ride. Coming back from Pressler's Garden, he made a proposal to her, and she refused, whereupon he swore she should comply. He knocked her out of the buggy and began to beat her and tear off her clothes. She screamed for help, and he put his hand over her mouth. A black woman called "Aunt Patsy" and her daughter ran to Rose, whereupon Brown jumped up and ran away, leaving the buggy and his hat and handkerchief. Rose's face and head were all scratched and bruised and cut. She stated that Officer Thorp, who had gone out to fetch the abandoned buggy and horse, as well as Brown's hat and handkerchief, had told her that she had better not make any charge against Brown.

Thorp said that on the afternoon of the incident, Brown had asked to use his horse and buggy, and he let him have it reluctantly, as Brown had been drinking beer very freely at the emancipation ("Juneteenth") picnic grounds. Not finding the horse in any livery stable the next morning, and learning that a loose horse and buggy was roaming around near Pressler's Garden, Thorp went out and found the horse drawing the buggy around through the bushes. The buggy was uninjured, and he found a revolver in it belonging to Officer Peck, and used by Brown the day before. He found Brown's hat at Aunt Patsy's house, which he brought to Brown, and took his horse and buggy home. He said that he did not tell Rosa that she had better not cast charges against Officer Brown.

Officer Brown emphatically said that the whole thing was a vile conspiracy, originated by a "brother officer" to ruin him; he said that the buggy turned over with him, that Rosa only gave one scream, that he offered her no violence whatever and that the story about an attempted outrage was concocted on the foundation of the bruises received by accidentally overturning the buggy. Brown was charged with assault with intent to commit rape on a woman of ill fame. Brown ended up pleading guilty and was fined ten dollars and costs.

Sometime after midnight on September 30, 1886, Edward Rousseau, a former Travis County deputy sheriff who was now running a saloon in Taylor in Williamson County, visited Blanche Dumont's *maison*. While there, he had some words with a girl called "Dasie," and picking up a spittoon from the floor, he struck her a fearful blow over the head, felling her. She was conveyed to Samostz's all-night pharmacy, where her wounds—a cut on the temple and one just below the right eye—were dressed. Officer Johnson promptly arrested Rousseau, and he gave bond in the sum of $150 on a charge of assault and battery. He was fined ten dollars and costs. Ironically, he was gunned down in his saloon just weeks later.

Master fakir Jeff Cain had a fancy for beating up the frail ones of color, as described in "Mixing the Colors." But whacking white girls gave him equal satisfaction. Jeff went to Blanche Dumont's house one Sunday night in September 1883 and began to raise cain in earnest. Several policemen went to the rescue. The next morning in court, Jeff pleaded guilty to a charge of assault and battery and was fined ten dollars and costs.

Jeff "frescoed the optic" of Josie Gilbert (gave her a black eye) on Saturday evening, July 26, 1884, and was arrested for aggravated assault and carrying a pistol. He was placed under a peace bond of $200. Cain was again arrested on July 28 on three charges, by Josie, for carrying a pistol on Saturday night and again on Sunday, as well as with threatening to do her serious bodily injury. The peace bond was forfeited, and a new one fixed at $1,000. The jury, after hearing the testimony and arguments in the first of the pistol cases, rendered a verdict of guilty and assessed the penalty at $50 and costs. Not to be outdone, Jeff charged Josie with being a common prostitute. The jury found a verdict of guilty and assessed her fine at $10 and costs.

Jeff Cain was up before the judge again on January 29, 1885. "It's getting to be a habit of Jeff's to answer to the roll call," the *Statesman* noted. This time it was on two charges—one for striking Ida Stotts and the other for disturbing the peace by drawing a knife on Gertie Hines. He spent $17.50 in both cases.

A Guy Town girl had to be able to protect herself. There was a grand ball at Bell's variety theater hall on the night of May 26, 1881, and the fun flowed until the wee hours of the morning. Miss Versey Clyde, who "boarded" with Miss Lillie Gibson, carefully concealed about her lithe, graceful form a very wicked-looking dirk, to be fully prepared for any emergency that might arise. While moving in the intricacies of the "German," the "racket" or some other dance then most fashionable, the weapon slipped from its fastenings and fell to the floor. Officer Chenneville, who was on duty at the time, saw it and arrested Versey for carrying concealed weapons, and she was fined twenty-five dollars and costs.

Catfights, of the woman-on-woman school, have long been a popular spectator sport, and Guy Town's *demimondes* did not disappoint. There were sounds of revelry down in Guy Town one January night in 1881 that soon turned into the muttered curses and unearthly yells of a first-class muss between the inmates of two of the prominent places of resort there. The two houses were jealous of each other, and the ruckus attracted the attention of the officers, who proceeded to scoop in all concerned. They were carried before the judge and, amid much weeping and untold grief, pleaded guilty and deposited the amount of their respective fines.

A gaggle of edified observers witnessed an intensely interesting row one morning in March 1881. Two of the females who flourished and prospered in Guy Town were having high words, and one of them cheerfully punched the head of the other with her fist. Hairpins, bangs, combs, skirts and slippers—to say nothing of well-rounded, sarcastic epithets—filled the air and contributed no little to the attractiveness of the great emotional, free and easy fight.

Annie Thompson and Millie Haley celebrated Thanksgiving 1882 with a fire fight, during which Annie struck Millie over the head with a lighted kerosene lamp, burning all her hair off and burning her face and neck terribly.

In a rumpus between some of the women at Sallie Daggett's one afternoon in June 1886, Josie Gilbert got badly cut in the neck when she fell against a looking glass during the mêlée and broke it. She gave Viola White a black eye. Josie and Viola, together with Viola's friend, Myrtle Wood, who also took part in the fracas without getting damaged, were arrested on the charge of fighting and disturbing the peace.

People in the neighborhood of Second Street, between Colorado and Lavaca, were startled to see a woman unmercifully clubbing the head of another woman on the afternoon of April 20, 1891. Mollie Smith was wielding the stick and Cora Scott receiving the blows. The scrap was caused by a love affair in which the green-eyed monster figured. Cora had gone to Mollie's house to upbraid her for what she considered false dealings in relation to their mutual lover. One word led to another until Mollie grabbed a stick about six feet long and one and a quarter inches square and smashed her rival over the head. When Cora ran, Mollie pursued her into the street, belaboring her until they reached the sidewalk, whereupon Cora fell to the ground from the effects of the blows.

The difficulty began in a rock house on Third Street near the corner of Lavaca, and Cora lay unconscious in front of it for nearly an hour before anyone was kind enough to carry the helpless sufferer to a friend's home on the next corner. Dr. Jones found that her skull had been badly fractured and indented and her left hand broken. The greater part of the time she was totally unconscious, with occasional intervals of semi-consciousness. Mollie was arrested for assault. Cora was conveyed to the hospital, where she eventually recovered, at least physically.

This was not Cora's first time to get the short end of the straw. Birdie Adams tried her hand in the artistic work of carving up Cora's countenance in January 1885. Birdie was charged ten dollars and costs for her cutlery work. Her "feller" footed the bill. Less than a month after her beating by Mollie, the barely recovered Cora tried to kill herself by taking a twenty-five-cent overdose of morphine. Dr. Richard Graves was summoned and, by a liberal usage of the stomach pump, succeeded in saving her life.

Sometimes the blows were "all in the family." Lizzie Williams, alias "Buzzard Liz," and Abe Williams, alias "Buzzard Abe," were mother and son. Abe had been in San Antonio for some time but returned to Austin around April Fool's Day 1893, since which time he had not treated his mother with the affection expected of a loving and devoted son. At about 8:45 p.m. on April 2, Abe went home and proceeded to beat his mother about the head in a manner most unmerciful. Her cries for help brought the night watchman at Christian & Crooker's lumberyard to her assistance, and as soon as he saw him, Abe started to run off. Two shots were fired after him, and he stopped and came back, meek and penitent. The watchman started to the police station with him but was soon met by Officer Peeples, to whom he turned over the prisoner.

An "Arabian quarter" that grew up in Guy Town in the early 1890s was viewed as an improvement on the established population. "During the past three or four years many dusky sons and daughters of Arabia have settled in Austin and they make a comfortable living peddling cheap jewelry and trinkets and doing odd jobs. Both men and women peddle and they tramp into the country for miles," reported the *Statesman* in September 1893.

> *They are congregated at the foot of San Antonio street where they have two small stores. Their living rooms, while somewhat crowded, as a rule are kept clean, and the women are tireless workers and do a deal of washing. Some of them are rather good looking and nearly all have pretty eyes. They use goat milk almost entirely and well kept nanny goats are staked in the back yards and milked several times a day. The Arabian quarter is a very quiet one and the police have little trouble keeping order down there. In religion they are Mohammedans and when in trouble cross themselves and upon their knees bow towards Mecca.*

Life in Guy Town was beginning to calm down, ever so slightly. The "good times" were moving east. By the time Guy Town by gaslight ended with the brilliant electric lighting system in 1895, bars on East Sixth Street were outnumbering those in Guy Town. The great fakirs were gone. And the name "Guy Town" was fading into the sunset.

CHAPTER 13

TURN OUT THE LIGHTS, THE PARTY'S OVER

By 1913, the vice district once called Guy Town was forty years old, and while prostitution still thrived there, the rollicking days of "feudin', fussin' and a-fightin'" were nearly twenty years gone. Despite the bluenoses' protestations that the district was responsible for a disproportionate share of Austin's criminal behavior, that honor actually belonged to East Sixth Street. Guy Town had matured into an otherwise pretty peaceful and orderly, though very poor, neighborhood with a predominately Mexican population, to the extent that it was often referred to as "Little Mexico." Walker Industries had chili and tamale plants there, where 15 percent of unskilled Mexicans worked.

The "city dads" had tried on a number of occasions, in vain, to defang Guy Town since 1870. After a surprisingly short battle launched on June 20, 1913, Austin became the first major city in Texas to shut its "reservation," at the stroke of midnight of October 1, 1913.

When Austin's city council passed an ordinance subjecting owners and keepers of bawdyhouses to fines between $50 and $100 and imprisonment on June 28, 1870, Austin had only a few whorehouses and a few dozen prostitutes, who were not included in the ordinance (prostitution was legal). But there was only one policeman patrolling the district, and the *Daily Republican* advised the city to call out the state militia if it expected to suppress prostitution. The call never went out. The madams and their girls were unimpressed; one of them bought a house just off Congress Avenue on July 1.

A petition from several First Ward citizens headed by James Simms was read at the March 10, 1874, city council meeting, asking for the suppression

Quality Mills. *From the* Social Survey of Austin, *issue 15, of* Bulletin of the University of Texas, *issue 273, William Benjamin Hamilton, University of Texas, 1913. Courtesy E.O. Wilson.*

of fandangos in the house of Charley Cooney. First ward alderman Cal Metz thought that there ought to be some ordinance fixing the time when fandangos should cease at night. He thought it was within the council's power to suppress these festivities and that they ought to do it. Alderman Mitchell suggested that fandangos be limited to one a week. Three or four times a week was a nuisance. Men who keep those houses ought to be compelled to go outside the city limits, where there was no authority to prevent them, declared Alderman William Brueggerhoff.

At the March 23 meeting, the council adopted an amendment to the city's misdemeanor ordinance, noting that "the city marshal is hereby authorized and instructed to suppress and close" all houses where lewd men and women or persons who have no visible means of support meet for the purpose of fandangoing and the like.

The city council passed an ordinance in November 1875 to prohibit dancing at houses of prostitution or where prostitutes congregate or where such house or place is attached or belongs to any drinking saloon; any party violating the ordinance would be fined not less than $5 and not more than $100. The fines were paid, and the dancing continued.

January 17, 1877, was a cold, damp and dreary day, but it was both an interesting and profitable one at the Mayor's Court. The day before, sixty-one complaints were issued against parties violating various ordinances. From the character of the prisoners arraigned before him, it appeared that a moral era was at last to be inaugurated in Austin. Some twenty or thirty of the frailest, if not the fairest, were there on the charge of plying an avocation detrimental to the grand moral standing of Texas's capital city. Bedecked and bedizened, they shone in robed splendors, and they relieved the city's dire necessities to the tune of ten dollars and costs per person. But this financial pass at principals in depravity was too full of success, at least in a financial point of view, to allow accessories, innocent though some might be, to go scot-free. Accordingly, prominent men and others not named by the *Statesman* were brought up on the charge of renting houses to women of ill fame. One excellent gentleman, full of piety and noted as a great moral teacher, then and there learned for the first time that he had wronged society on the question of rents. This good man protested innocence and, disgusted with his own loose ways of driving a trade, pleaded guilty and hushed the matter up with fine and costs.

By the mid-1880s, an increasing number of city leaders and citizens had given up on the idea of prohibiting prostitution in favor of regulating it. In June 1887, the city council, acting on a petition from a group of citizens living on the edges to Guy Town, was considering passage of an ordinance that would confine houses of ill repute to defined bounds (Pine/Fifth Street to the north, Colorado Street to the east, Guadalupe Street to the west and the Colorado River to the south).

However, the *Statesman* warned:

> *Here the council is tampering with a subject that has generally surpassed the legislative wisdom of the great cities in this and other countries. A good many years ago the city of St. Louis attempted not merely bounding but the extinction of the evil. In this state the city of Houston some dozen years ago tried the same thing. Other cities have assayed to take hold of and throttle the social monster. But all these attempts have proved unsuccessful. Municipalities that have undertaken the extirpation or the absolute circumscribing of the ulcer that has, from time immemorial, eaten into the social body, have had to abandon the reform and leave the malady about where they found it. Probably the wisest thing that can be done is the plan adopted in Paris, the most refined city in the world. This is simply to regulate, by a watchful surveillance, an evil that cannot be destroyed as long as human nature remains what it is. In Paris and other European cities*

the license system is in vogue, which while legally recognizing, also holds prostitution responsible for damage.

Incident to this system is medical scrutiny and police regulation that render the evil the least hurtful possible. But should this system not be here adopted, we cannot, even though it be in doubt of much success, but wish the present attempt to repress and regulate this evil the greatest good it can accomplish. And if nine of the ten wards of the city can be saved from contamination, these sections will be benefited and this social curse, in its then limited sphere, can be the more closely watched, and its abuses the quicker and more effectively corrected.

An ordinance that would prohibit the rental of property outside Guy Town for the purposes of prostitution was debated for several weeks, and the city dads passed it by a twelve to six margin, but Mayor J.W. Robertson vetoed it because it condemned valuable private property to the purposes of prostitution, thus extending "license and recognition" to an immoral practice. Enough aldermen reversed their earlier vote to uphold Robertson's veto, and the idea of legally regulating prostitution was abandoned.

What the city dads could not accomplish, vigilantes threatened to do. Starting after the Civil War, vigilante groups commonly called "white caps" sprang up across the country whose self-declared duty was to discipline and otherwise put the fear of God into men and women of questionable morals, such as drunkards and prostitutes. Their tactics resembled those of the Ku Klux Klan. While Austin was largely free of vigilante activity, a local gang of white caps struck Georgia Fraser's house in the predawn hours of January 20, 1893. That morning, when Madame Fraser's inmates arose, they were somewhat surprised to find a white marble tombstone in the form of a cross set up in the backyard bearing the following inscription:

In Memoriam.
For
Bob Smith,
Pearl Roland,
Georgie Frazier,
Assassinated.
We Have Enough.
Leave.
Died
January 23, 1893

The stone had been stolen during the same night from Adkinson's marble yard on West Pecan Street. The inscription was placed on the polished marble with black paint, completely ruining it. It was not the work of a slouch but betokened the hand of a skilled artist, the scrollwork and lettering being beautifully executed.

Bob Smith, who had a gambling establishment running on the second floor of his building on East Sixth, was said to be the Austin correspondent of Kansas City's *Sunday Sun* paper, and Pearl and Georgia were accused of furnishing Smith with tips, which they emphatically denied, asserting that they had never furnished the *Sun* with a single item. They claimed that they felt confident of the identity of the perpetrators of the deed and, in defiance, said that if they had any regard for their own safety, they ought to let the matter drop where it stood and not attempt to carry it further.

As an aside, Smith was arrested on July 30, 1893, charged with cutting and destroying many of Pearl's dresses and other wearing apparel. Smith was jealous of Pearl, who had an eye for bright uniforms and good-looking soldiers, and she and Smith had some words. He threatened to destroy her clothes if she went to Dallas, something she said she was going to do but didn't.

Some time after, upon going to her room, she found several of her finest silks and satins badly cut and slit, and half a dozen dresses were put on exhibition at the station, showing the savage work of a knife. Three of her hats and a skirt or two were also cut, the hats being ruined. Smith declared that he was innocent. The jury begged to differ.

Life in Guy Town bumped and grinded along as before. On the morning of Wednesday, September 19, 1894, Mayor John McDonald instructed City Marshal Jim Lucy to "sit" on all the houses of ill repute in Austin, "lock, stock and barrel," between then and the following Monday. He further commanded that every known harlot in the city after the following Monday be arrested and fined every day she remained. The mayor would exert every effort to see that Austin was purged of these women.

Why the sudden rampage? He admitted that he had no idea of the evil until he had a case in court with reference to those famous precincts; there were thirty or forty young men as witnesses, and they showed such familiarity with all the doings of these joints that the mayor concluded to sweep them out of town entirely. "Another thing I would like to do," said the mayor, "is to have the city council pass an ordinance making it a finable offense for any man, old or young, to visit any of these establishments."

When it became known on the streets that the mayor had gotten out the threshing machine and was getting it in active operation, some speculations were made as to whether the order could be enforced. One or two of the "landladies" owned the houses in which they lived, and the question then arose: could the city police force them to shut up shop and leave their property?

Mayor McDonald had undertaken more than he could accomplish. He could have the keeper of a disorderly house arrested and fined every day of the year, but he could not by his "*Ipse dixit*" (an unsupported statement that rests solely on the authority of the individual who makes it) drive the keepers of these houses out of their houses. Prostitution continued to be permitted but not regulated. It was understood that the women and the houses were to maintain a relatively low profile.

There was one more unsuccessful attempt to regulate prostitution in 1904. By that time, the Progressive movement had gathered steam, with the goal of improving society by strengthening and enhancing the family, the foundation stone of American society. Prohibition and the war on the white slave trade were key weapons in the Progressives' fight. By 1913, the Progressive movement had achieved critical mass; the Anti-Saloon League first publicly appealed for a prohibition amendment. About half the country was already dry, thanks to local option laws.

At the same time, Christian crusaders in cities across the country, including Austin, were working to shut down their red-light districts. Reverend Robert "Fighting Bob" Shuler led Austin's Guy Town shutdown campaign. Shuler came from Temple, where he had waged an aggressive verbal war on "Booze Government." He took over as pastor of Austin's University Methodist Church in 1912. His first entrance into his church was pure theater: striding down the main aisle carrying his cheap battered suitcase and hat during the middle of Sunday service, bounding up to the pulpit, introducing himself and launching into a fiery sermon condemning congregation members for their sins. In 1913, he began attacking Guy Town and prostitution in general in newspaper essays and dozens of sermons.

Austin's anti-prostitution campaign was driven by, first, the perceived extent and evils of the "white slave trade"; second, the horrors of venereal disease, which was quite common among Austin high school and college students, as well as adults; and third, Guy Town's danger to University of Texas (UT) students. Shuler said that he had counted as many as 100 UT students on a single evening in Guy Town. UT's total enrollment was just over 2,300 at the time.

The people of Texas, whose taxes supported the University of Texas, were, the *Austin Church News* declared, demanding that "Austin furnish a more wholesome environment in which to train their sons and daughters. The

Brackenridge Hall. *Author's collection.*

travesty upon enlightenment of mind and nobility of character was everywhere apparent, when the Capital City of Texas was the center of what, because of its unassuming exterior and convenient location, had been frequently designated as the most pernicious reservation of any city of the entire South."

In the hotly contested statewide 1881 election to determine where the new University of Texas would be located, many of the towns and cities competing with Austin had pointed to the existence of Guy Town as reason enough not to locate the university here. It would be too great a temptation to the cream of Texas youth. And sure enough, a warm and intimate relationship developed between the university's male student body and the giddy girls of Guy Town. It was a relationship so close that Mollie Reeves and Ola Lindsey made a trip to Brackenridge Hall on May 26, 1892, to visit some of their boys. After the police received a telephone call that "two white prostitutes were prowling about the premises and that they refused to leave upon being told so to do," Officer Gibson went out and arrested the girls. They were charged with vagrancy and lodged in jail. Mollie was fined ten dollars, while the vagrancy charge against Ola was dismissed.

While the Shuler-led crusade was as hot as the summer weather, many prominent Austin men opposed shutting down the district, and one madam, Pearl Yoe, was confident enough to begin purchasing $18,000 in additional tenderloin property in August.

Mayor A.P. Wooldridge was bent on eliminating Austin's "pest places" and called a meeting of the Austin City Council on September 9 to close Guy Town once and for all. Debate among council members was heated. Councilman Haynes spoke in favor of the "reservation" system for containing municipal vice:

> *While I have great respect for our ministers, I regret to say that in my opinion the fair name of our beautiful city has been sullied, and more harm done our educational institutions and the morals of the young by the many suggestive expressions used in the campaign of the past few weeks than has been done by the segregated district during its existence.*
>
> *I believe it is necessary to segregate moral vice as it is to segregate small pox or any other disease, and the district, in my opinion, is the safety valve of any large community—and in those cities where the district has been abolished conditions have become infinitely worse, the habitués of the district, both male and female, being scattered in every part of the city with no red light danger signal displayed.*
>
> *Admitting, however, that we could drive the unfortunate women of the district from the city entirely—which, in my mind, is impossible, conditions would then prevail that no good citizen would like to contemplate.*
>
> *The result of the campaign waged by the ministers will, of course, be of great benefit to the denominational schools of other Texas cities, as many parents will, no doubt, be impressed with the false idea that Austin is worse than Sodom and Gomorrah and entirely unsafe for their children.*

Councilman Anthony next said that he had "studied the question before us since entering my duties as a Councilman. I have talked with good, honest, upright men; men who I would believe to be square and I have yet to find one of many coming to me with the opinion that segregation is not a good thing. I have also talked to a minister who expressed to me that he was in favor of segregation."

"Who was that minister?" asked one of the ministers present.

"I wouldn't say I had talked with one if I had not," shot back Anthony. "I have his name, but I hardly think what he had told me in private should be repeated by me here if I was to mention his name. I believe that would be unfair, but I have his name and could make it public if I deemed it wise."

Mayor Wooldridge said that he was not a brute; he wished to give the women in the district until October 1 to vacate or lead a life anew. "They are to be pitied, some of them. Yet are we to stand by and see those women continue to enter those doors of hell from which they cannot return," he said with rising voice. He then quoted the inscription over the door leading to hell from Dante's *Inferno*: "All ye who enter here leave hope behind." The mayor opined that many of the fallen women would return to normal living if given an opportunity.

Wooldridge came up with a cleverly phrased resolution that forced each councilman to sign it or possibly face impeachment proceedings for not "agreeably" performing his duties. The resolution passed unanimously, and Wooldridge ordered closure by October 1. The madams responded to the looming shutdown, according to William Anderson, by staging a grand ball—not in protest but rather in surrender. According to those present, it was a spectacular affair.

The scene on the evening of September 30 was one of desolation. Only a few places would admit any but those who had been frequent visitors in the past. In at least one house not even a candle was lit. Midnight came. Music ceased, lights went out, stealthy figures lurked in the shadows as they moved homeward and the restricted district of Austin was closed. Some inmates of the houses stayed until the end; others left earlier on the outbound trains.

In one notorious Mexican resort, there were a few rolls of matting. Two or three cardboard boxes containing personal effects were in one room. A piano was in one corner. Not even a curtain was to be seen. Four women sat on the floor waiting for midnight.

In another place, all windows were open, and the lights shone brightly. The entire interior could be seen, but not a rug was visible. One lone woman of the underworld leaned against a doorway looking out on the drizzly evening. The house's contents consisted of a trunk placed in the center of the floor of one room.

In one or two houses, the lights burned and music was heard, but none entered the front door. Occasionally, a carriage drove to the side door, and the occupant was cautiously admitted. Before 9:30 p.m., a policeman told all the women that "at 12 o'clock the music must stop and the lights must be out." He then saw that all saloons in the district were closed on time.

All day on the morning of September 30, vans backed up to the doors of the houses and loaded furniture. All day and night, madams and inmates were catching trains to leave the city. Many who admitted that they lived off the gains of the women also left with them. A few declared that they would remain. The women who had property interests could stay a short while until their houses were disposed of, but there could be no further violation of the law in doing so; none offered to resist when the last moment came.

There was order and quiet in the larger places, but the dives presented scenes of uproar and disorder. Several general mêlées were narrowly averted, and it frequently seemed that the police would have to be called to settle individual quarrels.

Several days later, the *Austin Tribune* announced that several arrests were expected the next day in connection with the anti-vice campaign. Nearly all the district's residents had left the city, and it appeared deserted, save for one place at which the arrests might be made: a house with a large sign for "Furnished Rooms" hung out. Chief Morris said that he would be closely watching the house.

At a UT men's mass meeting on October 11, to demonstrate that the students of the University of Texas stood for clean living, a majority of the seven hundred students in attendance voted to endorse the closure of Guy Town, recognizing that prostitution was irreligious, immoral, unsanitary and contrary to the law and pledging their moral support to the police and citizens of Austin. It was hoped that this action would do much to correct certain misunderstandings concerning the moral plane of university men.

There is at least one recorded instance of a "soiled dove" who lent credence to the mayor's belief that many of these women would return to normal lives if given a chance. The *Tribune* was discreet enough not to mention her name but did note that on October 11, in the Fifty-third District Court, a former inmate of one of the houses secured a divorce from her husband, alleging abandonment and cruel treatment. She testified that they were married when he brought her to Austin and placed her in one of the houses. Shortly after bringing her to Austin, he left her and went to Dallas and had since forced her to give him money. When the anti-vice crusade started, she realized that she could do better and left the house, shortly thereafter securing a position as a nurse in an Austin family and filing for divorce.

Five of the doves were married before the final curtain fell and went on to lead normal, happy, familial lives, according to William Anderson.

Guy Town's demise not only put many hardworking women in search of new horizons, it also put paid to young T.C. "Buck" Steiner's first business, selling pencils. The whores were his best customers, he rued decades later. Born in 1899 in what is now south Austin, Buck Steiner was one of the most colorful characters in Austin history and its all-time horn doggiest. Patriarch of the Steiner Rodeo Company empire and made famous in Jerry Jeff Walker's song about Charlie Dunn, who made cowboy boots at Buck's Capital Saddlery, Buck always said he lost his virginity at age 6, having traded a sandwich stolen from his brother's lunch pail for his rite of passage. Buck lived to be 101, and although he probably didn't die with his pants down, it would not have been for lack of trying. He once declared that on a drive to Fort Worth, he couldn't make it past Waco without stopping for a little fun. While at the height of

He: I'll be around tonight and teach you how to make love properly.

She: How many other girls are taking the course?

Left: "Love Lesson" (1928). *Author's collection.*

Opposite: "Halloween Comes On—The Sport's Begun." *From* The Coyote, *University of Texas student humor magazine, October 1912.*

his fame as a rodeo star in the early 1930s, he coupled up with Sally Rand, the bubble dance sensation at the 1933 Chicago World's Fair, and the head wrangler of the "Nude Ranch" traveling show.

In early November 1913, Mayor Wooldridge proclaimed the success of the campaign against prostitution and noted that the campaign originated and was carried on largely out of regard for the students of the University of Texas; he wanted the backing of those "noble, intelligent young men." Some of them cooperated, but others took to phoning the president of the Anti-Vice League late at night with false reports of new prostitutes in town.

Ironically, the sexual revolution at UT was "a-borning" as Guytown was "a-dying," despite the university administration's futile efforts to keep surging young hormones in check.

It turns out that folks like Councilmen Haynes and Anthony were right: closing Guy Town and voting in Prohibition in 1918 didn't keep UT students from getting drunk and having sex. With the advent of the Roaring Twenties, UT boys *and* girls were guzzling "New Braunfels No. 4" together and petting one another in places a dog wouldn't approve. Only fifteen years after Guy Town shut down, they were dancing to the Ben Pollack Orchestra's "Keep Your Undershirt On," as Scrappy Lambert crooned:

> *Oh baby, I'm just full of sex.*
> *Go on and pet me for heaven's sake.*
> *But don't get excited, keep your undershirt on.*

And the streetwalkers were now called "call girls."

INDEX

ABOUT THE AUTHOR

Richard Zelade is a collector and teller of Texas tales: heroes, outlaws, fussin' and feudin', real tales, tall tales, small tales, music, whores, wars, sex, drugs, roll and rock, eccentricities, legends, characters, roadside attractions, tasty grub and more.

Zelade was born on May 25, 1953, in Brazoria County, Texas. He received a BA from the University of Texas–Austin in 1975, with honors and special honors in history. He began writing professionally in 1976, and his work has appeared in *Texas Parks &*

Wildlife, *Texas Monthly*, *People*, *Southern Living*, *American Way* and many other publications. He is the author of several guidebooks, including *Hill Country, Central Texas* and *Austin*.

A multidisciplinary historian, Zelade studies Texas geology, weather, geography, flora, fauna and ethnic folkways, including the medicinal and food uses of native plants.

Visit us at
www.historypress.net

....

This title is also available as an e-book